Only Poor Dad
(A Journey of Faith, Resilience, and Purpose in the Pursuit of True Wealth)

AFJAL KHAN

Copyright © 2024 Afjal Khan

All rights reserved.

ISBN: 9798346638537

DEDICATION

To the dreamers who dare to build a life beyond circumstance,
To the believers who hold faith as their compass,
And to the resilient souls who persevere with purpose.
This book is dedicated to those who walk the path of ambition with humility,
who honor their roots even as they reach for the stars,
and who find strength in the wisdom of family and faith.
May this story remind you that true wealth lies in the heart,
in the kindness we show, and in the legacy we leave behind.
And to my own family, whose love, values, and guidance continue to be my greatest blessings—
This is for you.

CONTENTS

Introduction *6*

Chapter 1: A Boy with Big Dreams *8*

Chapter 2: The Pursuit of Music *18*

Chapter 3: Faith and Purpose *34*

Chapter 4: Facing Reality *43*

Chapter 5: Discovering New Paths *57*

Chapter 6: The Fruits of Faith and Resilience *68*

Chapter 7: A Father's Wisdom *80*

Chapter 8: Building a Dream *87*

Chapter 9: The Road to Success *95*

Chapter 10: Gratitude and Giving Back *102*

INTRODUCTION

Welcome to the world of *Only Poor Dad*, a fictional tale of dreams, resilience, and purpose. Though this story mirrors real-life struggles and triumphs, it is a crafted narrative—a journey imagined, yet resonant with universal truths. This book is a work of fiction, a story that pulls from the elements of life many of us know: the complexities of ambition, the pull of faith, and the desire to create a life that is greater than our beginnings.

Our protagonist, Afjal Khan, grows up in a modest family with few financial resources but an abundance of love and moral strength. His father, a man with little material wealth but abundant wisdom, labors in America to provide for his family back in Pakistan. Afjal's life begins in a small village, where dreams are scarce but the will to achieve them is powerful. This story is not about wealth itself, but the internal journey toward defining one's success in a way that honors family, faith, and personal integrity. Inspired by the tenets of Islam and the cultural foundations of his family, Afjal's story captures a universal journey to find purpose and meaning beyond material gains.

As Afjal grows, so too do his ambitions. First enchanted by music, he ventures into a path that blends passion with the reality of financial hardship. It is a story of persistence and ingenuity: when resources are scarce, Afjal improvises, using a simple laptop and the basic tools at his disposal to produce music and share his voice with the world. His passion is undeniable, but soon, he finds himself at a crossroads. The wealth he seeks seems to clash with the tenets of his faith, forcing him to question whether his dreams align with his values.

Throughout his journey, Afjal is guided by the wisdom of his mother and father, voices that echo with principles of humility, patience, and faith. His parents' teachings remind him that success is more than just accumulating wealth; it is about using one's blessings to uplift and serve others. These values, deeply rooted in Islamic teachings, become the compass guiding Afjal through moments of doubt, temptation, and despair. His journey becomes not only one of personal growth but of spiritual development, as he learns that wealth is a trust and a test—a responsibility that must be managed with integrity and compassion.

Afjal's story is a deeply human one. Though fiction, it reflects the trials and rewards of striving for success while staying true to one's principles. For those readers familiar with the challenges of balancing ambition with faith, this story will resonate deeply. Afjal's journey reminds us that our lives are shaped not only by the paths we choose but by the values we hold. As he ventures into new fields, from music to business, and navigates the modern-day trials of entrepreneurship, Afjal learns that true success is not about what we achieve but about who we become in the process.

We invite you to walk this journey with Afjal, to witness his struggles, his joys, and his revelations. This book is a tribute to the universal human experience—a fictional yet relatable story about the pursuit of dreams, the strength found in faith, and the enduring power of family. *Only Poor Dad* is not just a story; it is an exploration of what it means to live a life of purpose, of humility, and of unwavering faith in a world often driven by material pursuits.

Let this book remind you that, no matter where we begin, no matter how humble our circumstances, each of us has the power to shape a life of meaning. Each of us can create a legacy of service, compassion, and love that far outweighs any material wealth.

CHAPTER 1: A BOY WITH BIG DREAMS

Beneath the quiet shadows cast by the setting sun, the earth took on a hue as if blessed by a painter's brush. I, Afjal, wandered along the familiar paths that edged our village, observing each stone, each blade of grass as if they, too, held secrets of resilience within their quiet forms. The world about me was humble yet alive, and I took heart in these small wonders, for they whispered of hidden strength—an enduring spirit that I sought to nurture within myself.

Though my heart was young, its beats echoed with a hunger that no feast could sate. I yearned not merely for bread to sustain my body, but for a chance to carve my own mark upon the vast and indifferent world. Such musings, to my mother, were as delicate as morning mist, fragile dreams that she sought to guide rather than quench. She, with words as gentle as a spring's whisper, would say, "Let thy heart be patient, for all gifts given by Allah require both the seed of effort and the rain of waiting." I pondered her words deeply, yet the embers within me flared too brightly to be so easily stilled.

In those moments of reflection, I would often find myself lost within the memories of my father, a figure whose presence was known only by letters and distant tales. My mind painted him as a man of iron will, who labored not for mere coins but for the promise of a future unseen. America was his battlefield, and we, his family, were the cause he held sacred. And though I could not yet understand the magnitude of his sacrifice, I felt a kinship, a call to honor his toil through my own acts of strength and ambition.

One evening, as I sat beneath the pale glow of a crescent moon, I heard the faint echoes of music drifting from the heart of our village. It was a melody simple and pure, unadorned by grand instruments yet as potent as any symphony. Drawn as if by an unseen hand, I rose and followed the sound to its source, finding a lone musician seated upon a worn mat, his fingers dancing over a stringed lute. His eyes were closed, his soul adrift within the notes he wove, oblivious to all but the language of his heart.

In that moment, I felt a stirring unlike any other. Here was a man who, through sound alone, expressed a world of joy and sorrow, hope and despair. Each note was a prayer, each chord a cry, as if he had gathered all the passions of life and poured them forth through his humble instrument. And I, a mere boy with no claim to wealth or fame, was entranced. It was as though Allah Himself had placed this man in my path, as a messenger to awaken a calling yet unknown within my heart.

Upon returning home, I found my mother by the firelight, her gaze steady as she mended our worn garments. I told her of the musician and the magic I had witnessed, my words tumbling forth with the fervor of newfound purpose. She listened, her hands still, her face softened by the glow of the hearth. "My son," she said, her voice as soft as a prayer, "Allah places in each of us a gift. But remember, a gift is not for one's own pleasure alone; it must serve a purpose beyond self."

Her words resonated within me, striking a chord as profound as any music. In that moment, I understood that if I were to follow this calling, it must be with humility, for a life devoted to mere ambition is a life without meaning.

Days passed, and yet the memory of that musician lingered within me, like a melody that refuses to fade. My hands, though empty, longed to hold an instrument, to feel the pulse of sound as it traveled from my heart to the world beyond. It was a yearning as pure as the first breath of dawn, a desire that spoke of purpose yet dared not name itself. But in our household, where each coin was precious, such dreams were luxuries that could not be afforded.

And yet, as if by divine decree, an opportunity arose. By means of small labors and the grace of Allah, I had managed to save a modest sum. It was little more than a pittance, yet in my hands, it felt as weighty as gold. With this treasure, I ventured to the marketplace, where amidst the stalls of spices and silks, I found a modest recorder. It was neither grand nor new, but to me, it was a portal—a way to weave my own melodies, however humble, into the tapestry of life.

Returning home with my prize, I took refuge in the grove at the edge of our village. There, surrounded by the trees that swayed with the breeze, I brought the recorder to my lips and let my breath shape the first tentative notes. The sound was soft, trembling, yet to my ears, it was as if the heavens themselves had opened to bear witness. Each note was a thread of my own making, a piece of my soul cast into the air, fragile yet determined to exist.

In that solitary moment, I tasted a sliver of the divine—a sense that my music, though modest, was a reflection of something greater, a humble offering to the vastness of creation. It was there, beneath the shelter of those trees, that I first felt the stirrings of a purpose that went beyond myself.

Oh, but the path of dreams is a road fraught with trials! My music, crude and simple though it was, soon drew curious eyes and wandering ears. My friends, Aman and Maqsood, who were to me as brothers, came upon me one day as I practiced in secret. They listened, their faces a mix of wonder and disbelief, for they, too, were sons of modest means, bound by the same limitations that had shaped my own life. Yet in their eyes, I glimpsed a spark—a recognition of the beauty that could arise even from humble hands.

Their presence lent strength to my resolve, for they did not mock my aspirations but instead stood beside me, offering words of encouragement. Aman, ever practical, spoke of ways to make my music known, while Maqsood, the dreamer, spun tales of fame and fortune that seemed both absurd and alluring. Together, they planted within me the notion that perhaps my music might reach beyond the boundaries of our village, a wild thought that both thrilled and terrified me.

And yet, in the quiet of my heart, a shadow lingered. For though ambition whispered sweet promises, I could not shake the words my mother had spoken—that a gift was a trust, not a trinket to be flaunted. I pondered this as I lay beneath the stars, the vast sky above reminding me of my smallness in the grand design of Allah's creation. Was it possible, I wondered, to chase a dream and remain true to one's faith? Could I walk the path of ambition without forsaking the values that had been instilled within me since birth?

Thus began a conflict within my soul, a battle between desire and duty that would shape my every choice. On one hand lay the promise of greatness, a chance to rise above the station of my birth and carve a name for myself. On the other lay the quiet call of faith, a reminder that true success is measured not by wealth or fame but by the contentment of the soul and the pleasure of Allah.

In the days that followed, I poured my energy into honing my skill, using my recorder as both teacher and companion. Each note, though flawed, brought me closer to an understanding of myself, as if music were a language that spoke directly to the heart. And yet, the more I played, the more I sensed the weight of my choices. For every step taken upon the path of ambition carried with it the risk of losing sight of that which mattered most—my faith, my family, and the values that had shaped me.

It was a lesson that echoed in my mind, a whisper from the depths of my soul that reminded me that all gifts, however great or small, are bestowed by Allah and must be wielded with humility. And so, as I continued to play, I made a vow—a promise to myself and to Allah that I would pursue this calling with a heart both bold and humble, seeking not only greatness but also grace.

With each note, I carved this promise into my very being, a silent prayer that my journey might lead me not away from my faith but closer to it, that I might find a way to honor both the dreams that burned within me and the values that had been entrusted to me by those I loved.

In the cool embrace of dusk, when the horizon blushed beneath the setting sun, my heart would often turn toward thoughts of my father. Though he was absent from our home, his presence lingered like the scent of spices after a feast, a quiet force that shaped my dreams and molded my hopes. I imagined him toiling in the land of America, a place that seemed as distant and strange as the stars above. I had only the letters he sent, and though his words were few, each line held a weight that burdened my heart with equal parts pride and sorrow.

In his absence, he had become to me both hero and myth, a man whose sacrifices I revered though I scarcely understood them. And as I reflected upon his journey, I felt within me the stirring of purpose—a call to honor his labor, to carry forward the torch of his dreams. Yet, my path was different, for while he carved his future with sweat and toil, I wished to shape mine with melody and sound, to bring forth a song from the silence that surrounded our lives.

But dreams of music were a luxury in a world where survival demanded pragmatism and resilience. Our village, though vibrant in spirit, was humble in means, and I often questioned whether my ambitions were a betrayal of the sacrifices my father had made. Could I, a son of simple birth, dare to reach beyond what life had laid before me? It was a question that haunted my nights, a dilemma that turned within my heart like a restless flame.

Yet, amidst these doubts, there was one constant—a strength that held me like the roots of an ancient tree. My mother, with her steady hands and unwavering faith, became my anchor. In her eyes, I saw a depth of wisdom that surpassed the words of any book, a knowledge born not of study but of survival, of love that endures even the harshest winters. She, more than anyone, understood the weight of dreams, for she bore them herself, though her life had left little room for their fulfillment.

One evening, as the stars began to shimmer above, I approached her, my heart burdened with questions I could scarcely voice. "Mother," I said, my voice a whisper in the silence, "do you think that dreams can change a man's fate?" She looked at me, her gaze soft yet fierce, as if she saw not the boy I was but the man I might become. "My son," she replied, her words like a gentle caress upon my soul, "dreams are not bound by fate, for they are the gifts of Allah, a glimpse of what might be if a man dares to believe."

Her words lit a fire within me, a resolve that would not be quenched by the hardships of life. For if dreams were indeed a gift, then who was I to cast them aside? And so, I clung to her wisdom, holding it close as a talisman against the fears that whispered in the quiet of my mind.

In the solitude of those dark nights, beneath the endless sky, I found myself grappling with thoughts of purpose and destiny. Life, as my mother often reminded me, was a test, a journey marked by trials meant to refine the soul, to draw one closer to Allah. And so, I pondered the meaning of my dreams, wondering if they, too, were part of this test, a way to teach me patience and resilience.

The road ahead seemed daunting, yet I was no stranger to hardship. From my earliest days, I had known the sting of hunger, the weight of worry etched upon my mother's face as she calculated the cost of each meal. And though I longed for more, I knew that my path would not be an easy one, that every step forward would demand sacrifice and strength.

But within me, there was a quiet confidence, a faith that had been nurtured by my mother's prayers and my father's labor. I believed, as she did, that Allah watched over us, that every hardship bore within it the seeds of its own reward. And so, I resolved to walk this path with patience, to trust in the wisdom that had been passed down to me through generations of struggle and survival.

Each night, as I lay beneath the stars, I would whisper a prayer, asking for guidance, for the strength to pursue my dreams without losing sight of what truly mattered. For in my heart, I knew that my journey was not for myself alone, but for all those who had come before me, for the family who had sacrificed so that I might dare to dream.

In the quiet moments before dawn, I would rise and make my way to the grove at the edge of our village, my recorder clutched tightly in my hand. There, amidst the trees that stood as silent witnesses, I would play, each note a prayer, a plea for purpose. The sound was raw, unpolished, yet it held a truth that words could not capture. It was as if the music, though flawed, was a reflection of my own soul, a cry that sought to reach beyond the limits of my world.

As the first light of morning crept over the horizon, I felt a peace that I had not known before, a quiet assurance that I was not alone. For though my path was uncertain, I sensed that Allah was with me, that He listened to the song of my heart as surely as He heard the prayers of my mother. And in that moment, I understood that my music was not merely a dream but a gift, a way to honor the life I had been given, to transform the silence of hardship into a melody of hope.

Thus, my journey began, not with a grand proclamation, but with a simple note played in the dawn's first light. It was a small beginning, yet within it lay the seeds of a purpose that would grow with each passing day. And though I did not yet know where this path would lead, I felt a quiet certainty that it was the path I was meant to walk, a road marked by both struggle and grace.

brighter with each passing moment. Yet, I kept my passion hidden, for I knew that dreams such as mine were fragile things, vulnerable to the harshness of reality. I practiced in secret, retreating to the grove whenever I could, pouring my soul into each note as if the world depended upon it. And in a way, it did, for my music had become my sanctuary, a refuge from the hardships that weighed upon my family and the uncertainties that haunted my heart.

Yet, even as I nurtured this gift, I was mindful of the lessons my mother had taught me. I knew that ambition, unchecked, could be a dangerous thing, a force that could lead a man astray from the values that held him steady. And so, I sought to balance my dreams with humility, to remind myself that my music was not for my own glory, but for the honor of Allah, who had bestowed this gift upon me.

It was a delicate balance, a struggle between desire and duty that would shape my every choice. For though I longed to rise above the poverty of my birth, I knew that true wealth lay not in fame or fortune, but in a life lived with integrity and faith. And so, with each note I played, I offered a silent prayer, a vow to remain true to the values that had been instilled within me, to honor both my family and my faith.

As my dedication to music blossomed, the world around me seemed to transform. I began to hear rhythms in the most unlikely of places—the quiet rustling of leaves, the soft patter of rain against the ground, even the gentle hum of the village as dawn broke over the rooftops. It was as though Allah had woven music into the very fabric of creation, a divine harmony that resonated within my heart, urging me to add my own voice to this symphony of life.

In the village square, where life bustled with the daily trades of our people, I would sometimes catch fragments of melodies sung by traveling musicians. Their voices carried stories of lands beyond our hills, tales of love and loss, of victory and despair. These songs seemed to open a door within me, revealing a world of possibilities, a realm where dreams were not confined by poverty or the boundaries of one's birth. I listened intently, drinking in every note as if it were a revelation, a glimpse of the life I longed to live.

Yet, even as my soul danced to the rhythms of these melodies, a shadow lingered—a reminder of the trials that lay ahead. For while music brought me joy, I knew that joy alone could not fill the emptiness of a hungry belly, nor mend the worn clothes that my mother carefully patched and mended each night. My ambitions, noble though they seemed, were mere fantasies in a world that demanded practicality and sacrifice. And so, my heart was torn between the call of my dreams and the reality of our humble life, a life rooted in survival and faith.

One evening, as I sat beneath the canopy of stars, my recorder resting in my hands, a thought struck me with a force that left me breathless. Was it possible, I wondered, that this passion, this love for music, was itself a test? A trial sent by Allah to measure my resolve, to see if I would use my talents not for selfish gain but for a purpose greater than myself. The idea filled me with both fear and wonder, for it hinted at a destiny beyond my understanding, a path that could lead me to honor or ruin.

I closed my eyes, allowing the silence to settle over me, and in that stillness, I felt a sense of peace, a quiet assurance that my journey, though uncertain, was guided by a hand far wiser than my own. I resolved to trust in that guidance, to let my steps be shaped by faith as much as by ambition. And though I knew that the road would be long and fraught with challenges, I felt a renewed strength, a conviction that I was not alone.

The stars above seemed to shine with a newfound brilliance, their light a reminder that even in the vastness of the universe, each life, each soul, held its own significance. I lifted my recorder to my lips and played a single note, letting it drift into the night like a prayer, a promise to honor this gift and the journey that lay before me.

As the days turned into weeks, my dedication to my craft deepened. Each morning, before the first light of dawn crept over the hills, I would rise and make my way to the grove at the village's edge, my recorder in hand. There, amid the whispering trees and the stillness of the early hour, I would practice, letting my soul speak through each note, each breath. It was a ritual as sacred to me as prayer, a communion with the beauty that lay hidden within the world and within myself.

But despite my passion, I was not immune to doubt. Often, I would find myself questioning the purpose of my journey, wondering if my dreams were mere vanity, a distraction from the duties that bound me to my family and my faith. These thoughts weighed heavily upon me, casting a shadow over my heart that no music could dispel.

One morning, as I played a tune that had been forming in my mind, I was startled by a soft voice behind me. "Afjal," it called, gentle yet firm. I turned to find my mother standing at the grove's edge, her face softened by a smile that held both pride and sadness. "I have watched you, my son," she said, stepping forward. "I see the passion that burns within you, the dreams that fill your heart. But remember, a gift is not truly a gift unless it serves others."

Her words struck me deeply, for they reminded me of the duty I owed not only to myself but to those who had given so much that I might dream. My father's labor, my mother's sacrifices, they were the foundation upon which my ambitions rested, and I knew then that my path would not be easy. For to honor my family and my faith, I would need to find a way to balance my dreams with humility, to pursue my calling not for fame or fortune, but for a purpose that went beyond myself.

That night, I lay awake beneath the stars, my mother's words echoing within me like a song that refused to fade. "A gift is not truly a gift unless it serves others." How simple, and yet how profound! In those words, I glimpsed a truth that I had longed for but could not name—a reminder that the pursuit of greatness, when divorced from compassion and service, is but an empty quest.

The dawn broke over the horizon, painting the sky with hues of gold and rose, and in that moment, I felt a clarity that had eluded me for so long. My dreams, my ambitions, they were not merely for my own advancement but for the betterment of those around me, for the honor of my family and the glory of Allah. With this understanding, I rose, feeling as though a weight had been lifted from my shoulders, a burden replaced by purpose.

In the days that followed, I approached my music with a renewed spirit, each note a prayer, each melody a tribute to the life I had been given. I played not for applause or recognition but for the quiet satisfaction of knowing that my music, however humble, could bring joy and hope to others. And in that simplicity, I found a peace that no ambition could ever provide.

As my music continued to grow, so too did my understanding of the world and my place within it. I began to see that life, in all its beauty and hardship, was a tapestry woven with both light and shadow, joy and sorrow. And though my path was uncertain, I took comfort in the knowledge that I was not alone, that Allah watched over me, guiding my steps even when I could not see the way.

One evening, as I returned from the grove, I found my mother waiting for me by the door, her face lit by the glow of the setting sun. She took my hand, her touch warm and steady, and led me to a small corner of our home, where a worn book lay upon a wooden shelf. "This," she said, her voice a whisper, "is the Quran, the words of Allah. Within these pages, you will find guidance, a light to carry you through even the darkest of nights."

I took the book in my hands, feeling the weight of it, the wisdom contained within its pages. And as I opened it, I was filled with a sense of reverence, a quiet awe that reminded me of my smallness in the face of the divine. For within these words, I sensed a truth that was both ancient and eternal, a knowledge that could guide me through the trials and tribulations of life.

In the days that followed, I began to study the Quran, seeking answers to the questions that filled my heart. And though I did not understand everything, I felt a peace that words could not describe, a certainty that Allah was with me, that He had a plan for my life that was greater than anything I could imagine. And in this faith, I found the strength to continue, to pursue my dreams with humility and purpose, knowing that my journey was but a part of a greater story, a story woven by the hands of the Almighty.

With each day, I grew in both skill and understanding, my music a reflection of the lessons I had learned and the values I held dear. And though my path was fraught with challenges, I felt a quiet confidence, a faith that guided me through even the most difficult moments. For I knew that my journey, though filled with trials, was a gift, an opportunity to honor my family and my faith, to pursue my dreams with a heart that was both bold and humble.

In the grove, where I practiced each morning, I felt a sense of peace, a connection to the beauty that lay hidden within the world and within myself. Each note, each melody, was a tribute to the life I had been given, a reminder that even the smallest voice could carry a message of hope and joy. And as I played, I felt a quiet assurance that I was not alone, that Allah watched over me, guiding my steps with a wisdom far greater than my own.

And thus, my journey continued, a journey marked by both struggle and grace, a path that led me ever closer to the life I sought, a life that was not only for myself but for all those who had come before me, for the family who had sacrificed so much that I might dare to dream. And in that journey, I found a purpose that went beyond mere ambition, a purpose that filled my heart with a peace that no wealth or fame could ever provide.

In the stillness of the early dawn, my heart found solace in the familiar weight of my recorder resting in my hand. It had become my companion, a small vessel through which my soul could speak the language it could not utter in words. And as the first light began to stretch its fingers over the earth, I would close my eyes and let the melody flow from my lips, a quiet offering to the morning itself. Each note seemed to rise like a breath of prayer, an expression of gratitude for the gift of life, however humble it was.

As my skill grew, so did my understanding of the purpose hidden within my music. It was not merely sound—it was a mirror, reflecting the struggles, hopes, and dreams that had shaped my life. With each note, I felt as though I were stitching together fragments of my soul, creating something whole and beautiful from pieces that had once felt scattered and small. And in that act of creation, I found a peace that could not be found in the world of things, a satisfaction that came not from what I held in my hands, but from what I could release from within.

Yet, even as I embraced this gift, a shadow remained, a quiet reminder that dreams alone could not feed or clothe a family. I was but one of many young men in my village, each of us bound by the same constraints of poverty, each bearing our own burdens and dreams. The reality of our lives demanded labor, sacrifice, and resilience, virtues that my father embodied with every day he spent toiling in a foreign land. And though my heart yearned to rise above these limitations, I knew that my journey would require not only talent, but also discipline and humility.

One morning, as I returned from the grove, I met Aman and Maqsood, my friends and brothers in spirit. They, too, carried dreams within them, dreams tempered by the realities of our village life. Aman was the practical one, his eyes always sharp, his mind ever weighing possibilities. Maqsood, on the other hand, was the dreamer, his heart as open as the sky, filled with visions of a world far beyond the horizon. Together, they were my companions, my guides along this journey of discovery.

Seeing the recorder in my hand, Aman raised an eyebrow, a hint of curiosity lighting his face. "Afjal," he said, his tone both gentle and probing, "what is it that drives you to play this music each day? What is it that you seek?" I paused, caught off guard by the question, for it was one I had often pondered but rarely voiced. I thought of my father, of my mother, of the quiet hope that lay like a seed within my heart, waiting to bloom.

"Perhaps," I replied slowly, choosing my words with care, "I seek a way to honor the life I have been given. To transform the silence of hardship into something beautiful, something that can bring joy to others." Maqsood nodded, his eyes distant, as if he too understood the longing that lived within me. "Then play, my friend," he said, his voice filled with quiet conviction. "Play not for fame or fortune, but for the joy that it brings. For in that joy, you may find the purpose you seek."

Their words stayed with me, a reminder that my music was more than a personal dream—it was a way to connect, to share, to build a bridge between my own heart and the hearts of others. And in that moment, I felt a renewed sense of purpose, a quiet determination to continue this journey, not for myself alone, but for all those who walked beside me, for all those who had given me the courage to dream.

As the days stretched into weeks, I found myself growing not only as a musician, but as a young man discovering his place in the world. Each morning in the grove became a lesson, not only in music but in patience, humility, and faith. For every note I played was an act of trust, a reminder that true purpose is often found not in reaching a destination, but in the journey itself, in the quiet steps that lead us ever closer to the life we are meant to live.

One evening, as I sat with my mother by the light of a single candle, I shared with her the thoughts that had been stirring within me. I spoke of my friends' words, of the joy I found in my music, of the hope that perhaps, one day, I might use this gift to bring honor to our family and glory to Allah. She listened, her face softened by a gentle smile, her eyes shining with a pride that needed no words. And as I finished, she took my hand in hers, her touch as warm as the sun upon the earth.

"Afjal," she said, her voice a whisper in the silence, "you have been given a gift, not by chance, but by purpose. Use it well, my son, and remember that true success is not measured by the applause of others, but by the contentment of your soul." Her words settled within me, a quiet flame that would guide me through the darkness, a light that would remain even in the hardest of times.

With each passing day, I carried her wisdom within me, a reminder that my journey, though uncertain, was blessed by the love and sacrifices of those who had come before me. And in that love, I found the strength to continue, to trust in the guidance of Allah, to walk this path with a heart both bold and humble.

Thus, my life became a balance of dreams and duty, of hope and humility. I continued to practice my music, each note a prayer, each melody a tribute to the life I had been given. And though my journey was only beginning, I felt a quiet confidence, a faith that sustained me through even the most difficult moments. For I knew that my path, however winding, was guided by a hand far wiser than my own.

In the days that followed, I began to sense that my journey was not for myself alone, but for all those who walked beside me, for the family who had sacrificed so much that I might dare to dream. And in that journey, I found a purpose that went beyond mere ambition, a purpose that filled my heart with a peace that no wealth or fame could ever provide.

As I played in the grove each morning, I felt a connection to the beauty that lay hidden within the world, a beauty that spoke of something greater than myself. And as I walked this path, guided by faith and hope, I found within me a strength that was not my own, a strength that came from the love and wisdom of those who had shaped my life.

And so, my journey continued, a journey marked by both struggle and grace, a path that led me ever closer to the life I sought, a life that was not only for myself but for all those who had come before me, a life that would honor my family, my faith, and the dreams that lay within my heart.

CHAPTER 2: THE PURSUIT OF MUSIC

The soul, once ignited by a spark of inspiration, knows no rest, no peace, until it has given form to that which stirs within. Such was the state of my heart after I tasted the joy of music, a joy that transcended words, a joy that whispered of purpose even in my modest life. The days that followed my first encounter with melody were filled with a restless energy, a desire to create and share, to give voice to the silent depths within me. Music had become my sanctuary, a place where I could escape the boundaries of poverty and taste, however briefly, the boundless freedom of the spirit.

Yet, I was not blind to the limits imposed upon me by the life I led. Music, though a gift, was not a necessity in our home, where every coin was counted, where every expense was weighed against our needs. My mother's hands, worn and calloused from years of labor, spoke of a life devoted to sacrifice, to survival. And I knew that in her heart, my dreams of music were but fragile things, dreams that could neither feed nor clothe us. Still, she did not quench my ambition, for she understood, in her quiet way, the yearning that had taken root within me.

In the dim hours before dawn, I would rise, slipping from our home with my humble recorder in hand, a token of my ambition. Each morning, as the world lay in silence, I would retreat to the grove, the one place where my heart could sing freely, unburdened by the gaze of others. There, I practiced with fervor, each note a step upon a path that I hoped might one day lead me beyond the confines of my life. It was a journey of discovery, a journey marked by both joy and struggle, for though my spirit soared, my skill was yet young and unrefined.

Yet, the journey of music, like all pursuits of the soul, demanded sacrifice.

Only Poor Dad

My heart yearned for a true instrument, a means by which I could give full expression to the melodies that lived within me. The recorder, though dear to me, was but a shadow of what I needed, and I knew that if I were to pursue this path, I would need more than a boy's dreams—I would need tools, knowledge, and, above all, patience. But patience is not an easy virtue for a heart filled with ambition, and I soon found myself wrestling with a desire that seemed, at times, to outstrip my means.

In those moments of doubt, I would recall the words of my mother, words that held within them the quiet wisdom of faith. "Allah provides for all creatures," she would remind me, her voice soft yet firm. "He gives to each according to their need, and if you seek with a pure heart, your needs will be met in His own time." Her words were like a balm upon my spirit, a reminder that my journey was not mine alone, that it was guided by a wisdom far greater than my own.

Thus resolved, I sought ways to bring my dreams closer to reality. By day, I labored in small tasks around the village, carrying water, mending walls, and running errands for those who could spare a coin or two. Each task, though modest, became a stepping stone, each coin a symbol of my commitment to a future that I could scarcely envision yet dared to hope for. And as I worked, I found within me a growing sense of purpose, a determination to forge my own path, however uncertain it might be.

After many days of labor, I held in my hand the sum of my earnings, a small collection of coins that I had saved with care. It was not much, yet to me, it felt like a king's ransom, a treasure earned by my own hand. With this modest fortune, I ventured to the marketplace, my heart pounding with anticipation, for I hoped to find there a tool that might aid me in my quest. The stalls were filled with goods, a dazzling array of colors and sounds that beckoned to the senses, yet my eyes sought only one thing—a laptop, a humble machine that might serve as the key to unlocking the music within me.

At last, I found it—a laptop worn by age and use, its surface scratched, its keys faded by the touch of countless fingers. It was no marvel of technology, no sleek device, yet to me, it was a treasure beyond price. With trembling hands, I placed my coins before the vendor, watching as he counted them with a look of bemusement. To him, this transaction was a mere exchange, but to me, it was a moment of transformation, a step toward a future that I could now begin to shape with my own hands.

As I returned home, the weight of the laptop in my arms was both a comfort and a challenge, a reminder that my journey was only just beginning. This tool, though simple, held within it the power to bring my dreams closer to reality, yet it also demanded discipline, commitment, and faith. I knew that the road ahead would not be easy, that each step would require both courage and sacrifice. But as I looked upon the modest machine in my hands, I felt a quiet thrill, a sense that I was, at last, taking control of my destiny.

In the quiet solitude of my room, with only the faint glow of a candle to light my way, I opened the laptop and took my first steps into the world of music creation. It was a world filled with mystery, a language that I had yet to learn, yet even in my ignorance, I felt a sense of belonging, a sense that this was the place where my heart could truly sing. The keys beneath my fingers were unfamiliar, the screen a portal to knowledge that lay just beyond my grasp, yet I was undaunted, for I knew that each obstacle was but another lesson, another step upon the path that I was destined to walk.

The night stretched on, and I lost myself in the process of discovery, exploring the sounds and rhythms that the laptop allowed me to create. My recorder lay beside me, a reminder of where I had begun, yet as I experimented with this new medium, I felt as though I had entered a realm of infinite possibility, a place where the limitations of my life could no longer hold me back. Each sound, each note, was a piece of my soul, a fragment of the dreams that had taken root within me, and as I worked, I felt a sense of fulfillment that I had not known before.

Yet, as the hours passed, fatigue began to settle upon me, a reminder that my journey was still one of struggle and endurance. My eyes grew heavy, my hands weary, yet I pressed on, driven by a force that I could not name but which compelled me to continue. It was as though the music itself had taken hold of me, urging me to push beyond my limits, to embrace the challenges that lay before me. And though my body ached with exhaustion, my spirit soared, lifted by the knowledge that I was, at last, walking the path that I had long dreamed of.

The days that followed were filled with both triumph and frustration, for though I had taken my first steps, the road ahead was fraught with challenges that I had not foreseen. The laptop, though a blessing, was a fragile tool, prone to fits of malfunction, its screen flickering and freezing at the most inopportune moments. Each glitch, each pause, was a reminder of the limitations that still bound me, a reminder that my journey, though blessed, was still rooted in the struggles of my life.

Yet, I refused to be discouraged, for I knew that every obstacle was a test, a trial meant to strengthen my resolve. My mother's words echoed within me, a constant reminder that faith was not merely a belief, but an action, a commitment to persevere even in the face of hardship. And so, with each setback, I returned to my work with renewed determination, each moment of frustration met with a prayer, each failure a lesson in patience and resilience.

My friends, Aman and Maqsood, would often visit me, their presence a balm to my weary spirit. They, too, had their own dreams, dreams that were no less worthy, no less noble, yet tempered by the same realities that shaped our lives. Together, we would speak of the future, of the paths we wished to walk, of the ways in which we hoped to bring honor to our families and glory to Allah. And though our dreams were different, we shared a bond, a kinship born of shared struggle and mutual support.

In those moments, I felt a sense of gratitude, a quiet joy that came not from my achievements, but from the knowledge that I was not alone. For though my path was one of music, and theirs one of different pursuits, we walked side by side, bound by a friendship that was as strong as any bond of blood. And in their presence, I found the strength to continue, to face each day with a heart that was both humble and hopeful, a heart that believed, despite all odds, that our dreams were worth the struggle.

The dawns grew into days, and each morning found me at the keyboard of my humble laptop, my fingers stumbling yet determined as they learned the art of digital music creation. It was a world as vast as it was intricate, and I marveled at the power that lay within my reach—a power to transform thought into sound, to give voice to the unspoken dreams that had long resided in my heart. Yet, for all its potential, this journey was not without its challenges. The laptop, though my most prized possession, bore the marks of time and wear, its screen dim and its keys worn, as if it, too, knew the weight of hardship.

At times, frustration threatened to overtake me. The programs I used would freeze or crash, and the sounds I created were often distorted, far from the pure melodies I heard in my mind. But each setback was met with patience, a virtue my mother had taught me to cultivate as carefully as one tends a garden. "In every trial, there is a blessing," she would remind me, her voice soft yet unwavering. "Allah tests those He loves, and through these tests, we find strength we did not know we possessed." Her words were a balm to my weary heart, a reminder that every obstacle was not a curse but a lesson, a chance to grow in both skill and faith.

As the days turned into weeks, my persistence began to bear fruit. The sounds I created grew clearer, the melodies more refined, each note a small victory, each rhythm a testament to the hours I had devoted to this craft. I found myself immersed in a world of possibility, a place where my dreams took on form and substance, where the limits of my life seemed to fall away. And though the journey was far from complete, I felt a quiet pride, a sense that I was, at last, beginning to walk the path that had been laid before me.

But the road to creation is not one of solitude alone, for no artist is an island, and every dreamer must seek the counsel of others. And so, one evening, as the sun dipped below the horizon and cast its final rays upon our village, I gathered my friends, Aman and Maqsood, to share with them the fruits of my labor. They, who had been my companions since childhood, were as curious as they were supportive, their eyes alight with the same wonder that had first drawn me to music.

Seated upon the worn mats in our humble home, I opened the laptop, its screen flickering to life as if in acknowledgment of the momentousness of the occasion. My hands trembled slightly as I pressed "play," and the room filled with the tentative melody that I had spent days crafting. It was a simple tune, unpolished yet sincere, a reflection of the journey that had brought me to this point.

For a moment, there was silence. Then Aman, ever the pragmatist, nodded thoughtfully, his expression one of quiet approval. "Afjal," he said, his voice steady, "this is but the beginning, yet already I can see where it might lead. You have something within you—a gift that deserves to be heard, a voice that can reach beyond the boundaries of our village." His words, though simple, struck a chord within me, a reminder that my dreams were not for myself alone but for all those who had supported and believed in me.

Maqsood, the dreamer, was less restrained, his face breaking into a grin as he clapped his hands together. "My friend," he exclaimed, "one day, the world will know your name! Your music will soar like the wind, carrying your heart's song to lands we have only imagined." His enthusiasm was infectious, and I felt a surge of hope, a sense that, perhaps, my dreams were not so distant after all.

Yet, even as my friends' words filled me with joy, a quiet voice within reminded me to remain humble, to remember the lessons my mother had taught me. For while ambition can drive a man forward, it can also lead him astray, tempting him to seek glory for its own sake rather than for the purpose it was meant to serve. And so, as I listened to my friends' praise, I reminded myself of the vow I had made—to pursue this path not for fame or fortune, but for the joy of creation, for the chance to honor the life that Allah had given me.

In the days that followed, I returned to my work with renewed dedication, each note a reflection of my commitment, each rhythm a testament to the patience and resilience that my journey demanded. I experimented with new sounds, new techniques, pushing the limits of my humble equipment, seeking ways to bring my vision closer to reality. And though the process was slow, filled with setbacks and frustrations, I found a peace in the act of creation, a joy that was both humbling and uplifting.

One evening, as I sat before my laptop, a thought struck me—a vision of a song that might capture not only my own journey but the journey of all those who had walked beside me, who had shared in my struggles and my dreams. It would be a melody of resilience, a tribute to the strength and hope that had sustained us, a reminder that even in the darkest of times, there is a light that cannot be extinguished. With a heart full of purpose, I began to shape this song, each note a reflection of the life I had known, each rhythm a tribute to the people and the faith that had guided me.

As the first draft of my song took shape, I felt a sense of anticipation unlike any I had known before. It was as if the music itself had come alive, as if it held within it a power that I could scarcely comprehend. Each note seemed to carry a message, a truth that spoke not only to my own heart but to the hearts of all who would one day hear it. And though I was but a humble musician, untrained and unrefined, I felt a responsibility to honor this gift, to bring forth the song in a way that would resonate with others, that would offer them the same hope and strength that had sustained me.

Yet, as the song grew, so too did my desire for tools that could do justice to the vision that had taken hold of me. My laptop, though beloved, was limited, its sound distorted, its capabilities stretched to the very edge of what it could handle. I knew that if I were to bring this song to life, I would need more than what I had—I would need a microphone, a set of headphones, equipment that could capture the nuances, the subtleties, the emotions that my humble laptop could not convey.

But these tools were not within my reach. They were costly, luxuries in a life where every coin was carefully guarded, where each expense was weighed against the needs of survival. And so, I found myself at a crossroads, torn between the desire to bring my vision to life and the reality of my circumstances. It was a test, a trial that demanded both patience and faith, a reminder that even the purest dreams must sometimes wait for their time.

In the days that followed, I wrestled with this dilemma, my heart torn between ambition and restraint. I longed to create, to give voice to the melody that had taken hold of me, yet I knew that the path I sought was not one that could be forced, that every step forward required both sacrifice and wisdom. And so, I resolved to be patient, to continue working with what I had, trusting that in time, Allah would provide the means to bring my dreams to life.

But the desire within me did not wane. It grew, as a flame grows when fed by the winds, a quiet fire that filled me with both hope and frustration. I spent long hours at my laptop, crafting my song with care, each note a step closer to the vision that had taken root within me. And though the journey was slow, filled with obstacles and setbacks, I found a peace in the act of creation, a joy that was both humbling and uplifting.

In those moments of frustration, I would remind myself of the lessons my mother had taught me, lessons of patience, of humility, of faith. "Allah tests those He loves," she would say, her voice a steady anchor in the storms of my heart. "And through these tests, we grow, we learn, we become the people we are meant to be." Her words were a balm to my spirit, a reminder that my journey, though challenging, was blessed, a gift that I had been entrusted with, a gift that I was bound to honor.

With each note, each melody, I felt a sense of purpose that went beyond myself, a calling that transcended the limits of my own ambitions. And though the road ahead was uncertain, I knew that I was not alone, that Allah walked beside me, guiding my steps with a wisdom far greater than my own.

The fire within me was both a gift and a burden, a force that propelled me forward yet also reminded me of the limitations that surrounded my life. I had music in my heart, a vision in my mind, but the tools to bring it to life seemed always just beyond my grasp. My laptop, though cherished, was a humble thing, struggling beneath the weight of my ambitions, its sound quality poor and its functionality limited. And so, I was left with no choice but to rely on patience, a virtue I was learning to cultivate like a gardener tends to the most delicate flowers, knowing that each bloom requires both time and care.

One evening, after another long day spent at the laptop, I found myself wandering the quiet paths of our village, the stars above a silent witness to my musings. My mind was heavy with thoughts of my song, of the dreams I had woven into its melody, dreams that seemed to reach toward the sky like the branches of a tree, yearning for sunlight. I wondered if they would ever see the light, if I would ever find the means to bring them forth into the world in a way that did them justice.

Lost in these thoughts, I nearly missed the sound of footsteps approaching from behind. Turning, I saw Aman and Maqsood, my friends and brothers in spirit, who had been my companions since childhood. They, too, had dreams, though perhaps not as grand or as burdened with ambition as mine, and in their faces, I saw a reflection of my own struggles. We were all, in our own ways, striving to find our place in the world, to rise above the constraints that life had placed upon us, to carve out a future that honored both our families and our faith.

Seeing the weight upon my shoulders, Aman placed a hand on my arm, his expression one of quiet understanding. "Afjal," he said, his voice gentle yet firm, "do not let this journey consume you. Remember that patience is as much a part of success as effort. Trust in the timing of Allah, for He knows what we cannot see, and He guides us even when the path is hidden." His words, though simple, brought me a sense of peace, a reminder that my journey was not mine alone, that it was guided by a wisdom far greater than my own.

Maqsood, ever the optimist, grinned and clapped me on the back. "One day, my friend," he declared, his eyes alight with hope, "you will look back on these days and laugh, for they will be but the first chapter in a story that the world will know. Your music will reach far beyond this village, beyond even this land, and people will hear your heart in every note." His words, though bold, filled me with a renewed sense of purpose, a quiet confidence that, perhaps, my dreams were not as distant as they seemed.

With my friends' encouragement in my heart, I returned to my work with a renewed spirit, each note a step forward, each melody a reflection of the journey that lay before me. I poured my soul into the song I was creating, a melody that spoke of resilience, of hope, of the faith that had sustained me through even the darkest of times. It was a song that was both mine and not mine, a reflection of the people who had shaped my life, of the love and sacrifice that had guided me to this point.

Yet, even as my music grew, so too did my desire for tools that could bring it to life in a way that did justice to its message. My laptop, though a faithful companion, was limited, its sound quality poor and its capabilities stretched to the very edge. I knew that if I were to bring this song to fruition, I would need more than what I had—I would need a microphone, a set of headphones, equipment that could capture the nuances, the subtleties, the emotions that my humble laptop could not convey.

But such tools were not within my reach. They were costly, luxuries in a life where every coin was carefully guarded, where each expense was weighed against the needs of survival. And so, I found myself at a crossroads, torn between the desire to bring my vision to life and the reality of my circumstances. It was a test, a trial that demanded both patience and faith, a reminder that even the purest dreams must sometimes wait for their time.

As the days turned into weeks, I continued to work with what I had, trusting that in time, Allah would provide the means to bring my dreams to life. I reminded myself that every great journey begins with a single step, that every achievement, however grand, is built upon a foundation of patience and perseverance. And though the road ahead was uncertain, I felt a quiet peace, a sense that I was walking the path that had been laid before me.

In the quiet of the night, as I worked on my song, I would pause and close my eyes, allowing the music to fill my mind, to take shape within my heart. It was a melody that spoke of hope, of resilience, of the journey that had brought me to this point. And though the tools I had were limited, I trusted that, in time, my vision would be realized, that the song I carried within me would one day reach the hearts of others, offering them the same strength and hope that had sustained me.

One afternoon, as I sat beneath the shade of an old tree, contemplating my next steps, I was joined by my mother, her presence a quiet reminder of the love and sacrifice that had shaped my life. She sat beside me, her hands folded in her lap, her gaze steady and calm. For a moment, we sat in silence, the gentle breeze carrying with it the scent of earth and life, a reminder of the world that lay beyond my dreams.

"Afjal," she said at last, her voice as soft as a prayer, "I see the fire within you, the drive that pushes you forward. But remember, my son, that even the strongest flame must be tempered by patience, for a fire that burns too hot will consume all in its path." Her words, though gentle, held a wisdom that pierced my heart, a reminder that my journey was not only about ambition but also about balance, about finding a way to pursue my dreams without losing sight of the values that had guided me since birth.

I nodded, absorbing her words, feeling their truth resonate within me. She, more than anyone, understood the weight of dreams, the burden of ambition, for she had borne her own dreams in silence, sacrificing them for the sake of our family, for the love that had sustained us through even the hardest of times. Her strength, her resilience, were gifts that I carried with me, a reminder that every achievement, every success, was built upon a foundation of love and sacrifice.

In that moment, I made a silent vow—to honor her sacrifice, to pursue my dreams with a heart both humble and strong, to use my gift not for my own glory but for the betterment of those around me. For in her eyes, I saw the truth of my journey, a truth that went beyond mere ambition, a truth that spoke of purpose, of a calling that transcended the boundaries of my own desires.

With a renewed sense of purpose, I returned to my work, each note a tribute to the love and sacrifice that had shaped my life, each melody a reflection of the journey that lay before me. And though the road was long, though the challenges were many, I knew that I was not alone, that I was guided by a wisdom far greater than my own, a wisdom that would lead me to the life I sought, a life that would honor both my family and my faith.

The journey of creation, I soon learned, was both a joy and a burden, a path that brought me closer to my dreams yet also demanded sacrifices I had not foreseen. My humble laptop, though cherished, was strained beneath the weight of my ambitions, its screen flickering and its keys unresponsive at times. Each technical flaw was a reminder of the limitations I faced, a challenge that tested not only my patience but my resolve. And as the days turned into weeks, my desire for more sophisticated tools only grew, a longing that was both practical and poetic, a wish to bring my vision to life with clarity and purpose.

But such tools required money, resources that I did not possess. And so, I sought ways to bridge the gap, to find a means by which I could continue my journey without losing sight of the realities that bound me. By day, I took on small tasks around the village, earning what little I could by helping neighbors with chores, carrying water, and running errands. Each coin I earned, though modest, was a symbol of my commitment, a testament to the lengths I was willing to go to pursue my dreams.

In the evenings, I returned to my work, my heart filled with both hope and weariness, a blend of emotions that I had come to know well. I would sit before my laptop, experimenting with sounds and rhythms, crafting melodies that spoke of resilience, of the strength that I had found within myself. And though my tools were limited, my spirit was not, for each note, each song, was a reflection of the journey that had brought me to this point—a journey marked by both struggle and grace, a journey that I was determined to see through to its end.

As I worked, I often thought of my mother, of the quiet strength she had passed down to me, a strength that was rooted not in ambition but in faith. Her presence, though silent, was a constant reminder of the love and sacrifice that had shaped my life, a love that had given me the courage to dream, even in the face of hardship. And though I could not yet see the end of my journey, I felt a sense of peace, a knowledge that I was not alone, that Allah walked beside me, guiding my steps with a wisdom far greater than my own.

One evening, as I sat by the light of a single candle, my eyes weary from the day's labor, I felt a sense of both satisfaction and longing—a satisfaction in the work I had done, a longing for the tools that might allow me to bring my vision to life more fully. I closed my eyes, allowing the music within me to take shape in my mind, a melody that spoke of hope, of resilience, of the journey that had brought me to this point. It was a song that was both mine and not mine, a reflection of the people who had shaped my life, of the love and sacrifice that had guided me to this moment.

In the silence, I found myself whispering a prayer, a quiet plea for guidance, for the strength to continue, for the resources that might allow me to bring my vision to life. And as I spoke these words, I felt a sense of peace, a knowledge that my journey was not mine alone, that it was guided by a hand far wiser than my own. I knew that every obstacle, every setback, was a lesson, a chance to grow in both skill and character, a reminder that true success is measured not by what we achieve but by the heart with which we pursue our dreams.

The days that followed were filled with both triumph and frustration, moments of clarity and moments of doubt. My friends, Aman and Maqsood, remained by my side, their presence a balm to my weary spirit, a reminder that I was not alone. They, too, had their own dreams, dreams that were tempered by the realities of our lives, dreams that spoke of resilience and hope. And though our paths were different, we shared a bond, a kinship that was as strong as any bond of blood.

Together, we spoke of the future, of the lives we hoped to build, of the ways in which we might bring honor to our families and glory to Allah. And though our dreams were different, they were united by a common thread—a desire to rise above the limitations of our lives, to find a purpose that went beyond mere survival, a purpose that spoke of hope and faith, a purpose that would carry us forward even in the darkest of times.

In the midst of my journey, I came to realize that patience, though often seen as a passive virtue, was, in fact, an act of great strength. Each setback, each delay, was a test, a challenge that demanded not only resilience but a trust in the timing of Allah. For though I could not yet see the end of my path, I believed, as my mother had taught me, that every struggle bore within it a hidden blessing, a lesson that would reveal itself in time.

One afternoon, as I sat beneath the shade of an old tree, contemplating the challenges that lay before me, I was joined by my mother, her presence a quiet reminder of the love and sacrifice that had shaped my life. She sat beside me, her hands folded in her lap, her gaze steady and calm. For a moment, we sat in silence, the gentle breeze carrying with it the scent of earth and life, a reminder of the world that lay beyond my dreams.

"Afjal," she said at last, her voice as soft as a prayer, "I see the fire within you, the drive that pushes you forward. But remember, my son, that even the strongest flame must be tempered by patience, for a fire that burns too hot will consume all in its path." Her words, though gentle, held a wisdom that pierced my heart, a reminder that my journey was not only about ambition but also about balance, about finding a way to pursue my dreams without losing sight of the values that had guided me since birth.

I nodded, absorbing her words, feeling their truth resonate within me. She, more than anyone, understood the weight of dreams, the burden of ambition, for she had borne her own dreams in silence, sacrificing them for the sake of our family, for the love that had sustained us through even the hardest of times. Her strength, her resilience, were gifts that I carried with me, a reminder that every achievement, every success, was built upon a foundation of love and sacrifice.

In that moment, I made a silent vow—to honor her sacrifice, to pursue my dreams with a heart both humble and strong, to use my gift not for my own glory but for the betterment of those around me. For in her eyes, I saw the truth of my journey, a truth that went beyond mere ambition, a truth that spoke of purpose, of a calling that transcended the boundaries of my own desires.

With a renewed sense of purpose, I returned to my work, each note a tribute to the love and sacrifice that had shaped my life, each melody a reflection of the journey that lay before me. And though the road was long, though the challenges were many, I knew that I was not alone, that I was guided by a wisdom far greater than my own, a wisdom that would lead me to the life I sought, a life that would honor both my family and my faith.

As I continued on this path, I found a sense of peace that I had not known before, a quiet assurance that my journey, though uncertain, was blessed. And though the tools I had were limited, my spirit was not, for each note, each song, was a reflection of the dreams that had taken root within me, dreams that spoke of hope, of resilience, of the strength that I had found within myself.

In the quiet of the night, as I worked on my song, I would pause and close my eyes, allowing the music to fill my mind, to take shape within my heart. It was a melody that spoke of hope, of resilience, of the journey that had brought me to this point. And though the tools I had were limited, I trusted that, in time, my vision would be realized, that the song I carried within me would one day reach the hearts of others, offering them the same strength and hope that had sustained me.

The path of music, I found, was as much a test of character as it was a journey of creation. My days were filled with moments of triumph and frustration, my nights with dreams that seemed to dance just beyond my reach. Each note, each melody, was a piece of my soul, a fragment of my dreams, yet the tools with which I worked were as humble as my means. My laptop, though cherished, bore the weight of its years, its screen flickering, its keys growing weary under the constant touch of my fingers. And though I longed for more—a microphone, a set of headphones, tools that could bring my vision to life—I knew that such luxuries were beyond my reach.

In the quiet hours before dawn, I would sit with my laptop, pouring my heart into the music, letting my soul speak through each note. It was a process both joyful and painful, a reminder of both the beauty of my dreams and the limits of my life. Yet, even as I struggled, I found a strange comfort in the act of creation, a peace that came not from the tools I lacked but from the journey itself, a journey that was both a test and a blessing.

One night, as I worked on a melody that had taken root in my mind, I felt a sense of restlessness, a desire to share my work, to let others hear the song that had become a part of me. And so, with a heart filled with both excitement and trepidation, I reached out to Aman and Maqsood, my friends and companions, who had walked beside me through every step of this journey. Together, we had shared our dreams, our hopes, our struggles, and I knew that they would understand the significance of what I had created.

When they arrived, their faces lit by the soft glow of the single candle that illuminated my room, I felt a surge of both pride and humility. They, too, had their own dreams, dreams that were tempered by the same realities that shaped my life, yet they had always supported me, always believed in me, even when I struggled to believe in myself. And as they settled onto the worn mats beside me, I opened my laptop, my hands trembling as I pressed "play," letting the melody fill the room, letting them hear the song that had become a part of my soul.

As the last note faded into silence, I glanced at my friends, their faces illuminated by the soft glow of the candlelight, their expressions a blend of awe and understanding. Aman, ever the pragmatist, was the first to speak, his voice steady, his words thoughtful. "Afjal," he said, his gaze steady, "this music is more than a song. It is a piece of you, a reflection of the journey you have walked, of the strength and resilience that have carried you through even the darkest of times."

His words struck a chord within me, a reminder that my music, though personal, was not for myself alone. It was a way to honor my journey, to give voice to the struggles and hopes that had shaped my life. And in that moment, I felt a sense of peace, a knowledge that my path, though difficult, was one that I was meant to walk, a path that would lead me not only to my dreams but to a deeper understanding of myself and the world around me.

Maqsood, ever the optimist, grinned, his eyes alight with excitement. "One day, my friend," he declared, his voice filled with conviction, "your music will reach far beyond this village, beyond even this land. People will hear your heart in every note, will feel the strength of your spirit in every melody." His words, though bold, filled me with a renewed sense of purpose, a quiet confidence that, perhaps, my dreams were not as distant as they seemed, that they were within reach if I had the courage to pursue them.

In the days that followed, I returned to my work with a renewed sense of determination, each note a step forward, each melody a reflection of the journey that lay before me. And though my tools were limited, my spirit was not, for each song, each sound, was a testament to the strength and hope that had sustained me, a reminder that, even in the darkest of times, there is a light that cannot be extinguished, a light that guides us toward our purpose.

But even as my dreams grew, so too did the challenges that lay before me. The road to creation was fraught with obstacles, each one a test of both skill and patience, a reminder that every achievement, every success, is built upon a foundation of struggle and sacrifice. And though I longed for more—for better tools, for the resources that might bring my vision to life—I knew that such things were not yet within my reach, that they would come only when the time was right.

In moments of frustration, when my laptop faltered or my melodies fell short of my vision, I would remember the words of my mother, her voice a steady anchor in the storms of my heart. "Allah tests those He loves," she would say, her gaze calm, her hands steady as she worked. "And through these tests, we grow, we learn, we become the people we are meant to be." Her words were a balm to my spirit, a reminder that my journey, though challenging, was blessed, a gift that I had been entrusted with, a gift that I was bound to honor.

And so, with each setback, I returned to my work, each note a reflection of my commitment, each melody a testament to the patience and resilience that my journey demanded. I experimented with new sounds, new techniques, pushing the limits of my humble equipment, seeking ways to bring my vision closer to reality. And though the process was slow, filled with moments of doubt and frustration, I found a peace in the act of creation, a joy that was both humbling and uplifting, a reminder that true success is measured not by what we achieve but by the heart with which we pursue our dreams.

One evening, as I sat before my laptop, a thought struck me—a vision of a song that might capture not only my own journey but the journey of all those who had walked beside me, who had shared in my struggles and my dreams. It would be a melody of resilience, a tribute to the strength and hope that had sustained us, a reminder that, even in the darkest of times, there is a light that cannot be extinguished.

The vision took hold of me, a melody that seemed to grow within my heart, a song that spoke of hope, of resilience, of the journey that had brought me to this point. It was a song that was both mine and not mine, a reflection of the people who had shaped my life, of the love and sacrifice that had guided me to this moment. And as I worked on this melody, I felt a sense of purpose that went beyond my own ambitions, a calling that transcended the boundaries of my own desires, a reminder that my journey was not for myself alone.

Yet, even as the song grew, so too did my desire for tools that could bring it to life in a way that did justice to its message. My laptop, though faithful, was limited, its sound distorted, its capabilities stretched to the very edge of what it could handle. I knew that if I were to bring this song to fruition, I would need more than what I had—I would need a microphone, a set of headphones, equipment that could capture the nuances, the subtleties, the emotions that my humble laptop could not convey.

But these tools were not within my reach. They were costly, luxuries in a life where every coin was carefully guarded, where each expense was weighed against the needs of survival. And so, I found myself at a crossroads, torn between the desire to bring my vision to life and the reality of my circumstances. It was a test, a trial that demanded both patience and faith, a reminder that even the purest dreams must sometimes wait for their time.

In the days that followed, I wrestled with this dilemma, my heart torn between ambition and restraint. I longed to create, to give voice to the melody that had taken hold of me, yet I knew that the path I sought was not one that could be forced, that every step forward required both sacrifice and wisdom. And so, I resolved to be patient, to continue working with what I had, trusting that in time, Allah would provide the means to bring my dreams to life.

And as I continued, I found within me a peace that I had not known before, a quiet assurance that my journey, though uncertain, was blessed. And though the tools I had were limited, my spirit was not, for each note, each song, was a reflection of the dreams that had taken root within me, dreams that spoke of hope, of resilience, of the strength that I had found within myself.

The days stretched on, each one blurring into the next as I poured my energy into my work, my passion, my calling. My humble laptop was my only instrument, yet through its worn keys and dim screen, I sought to bring forth the sounds that lived within me. Each evening, after my daily labor, I would return to the familiar glow of its screen, my fingers aching yet my spirit renewed. For in each note, each rhythm, I found a piece of myself, a reflection of the journey I was walking, a path both daunting and exhilarating.

But even as my skills grew, as the melodies took on form and shape, the desire for better tools gnawed at my heart. My music was like a river held back by a dam, its potential restrained, its beauty confined by the limits of my equipment. I could hear the songs within me, the complexity of their notes, the richness of their harmonies, yet what emerged was but a shadow, a mere echo of the vision that lived in my mind.

One night, as I wrestled with these thoughts, I found myself thinking of my father. He, too, had labored within constraints, leaving his homeland to seek a future in a foreign land, sacrificing his comfort, his companionship, for a vision that was as much for us as it was for himself. His life had been a testament to the power of resilience, a reminder that even the loftiest dreams required sacrifice, patience, and unyielding faith. And as I sat in the glow of the candlelight, I felt a kinship with him, a connection that spanned the distance between us, a reminder that, though we walked different paths, our struggles were bound by a common purpose.

The thought of my father brought a sense of peace, a quiet reminder that my journey, though challenging, was a continuation of his own, a testament to the strength and hope that had sustained our family through generations. And though my heart still longed for the tools that might bring my vision to life, I resolved to honor his example, to continue with what I had, to let patience be my guide, to trust that in time, Allah would provide the means to fulfill the dreams that had taken root within me.

As the weeks passed, my commitment deepened, each day a step forward, each melody a reflection of my journey. My friends, Aman and Maqsood, became my constant companions, their support a balm to my weary spirit. Together, we shared our hopes, our dreams, our fears, bound by a friendship that was as strong as any bond of blood. They, too, had their own aspirations, dreams tempered by the realities of our lives, yet they had always believed in me, always encouraged me to pursue my calling, even when the road seemed fraught with obstacles.

One evening, as the three of us sat by the fire, the warm glow casting shadows upon our faces, Aman spoke, his voice filled with a quiet conviction. "Afjal," he said, his gaze steady, "your music is a gift, a voice that can reach beyond the boundaries of our village, beyond even this land. Do not let the lack of resources hold you back, for true talent, true passion, transcends the limits of what we possess."

His words struck a chord within me, a reminder that my journey was not defined by the tools I lacked but by the heart with which I pursued it. And though my path was one of struggle, I knew that each note, each melody, was a testament to the strength and resilience that had brought me to this point. For in every obstacle, I found a lesson, a chance to grow, to learn, to become the person I was meant to be.

Maqsood, ever the dreamer, leaned forward, his eyes alight with excitement. "One day, my friend," he declared, "the world will hear your music, will feel the strength of your spirit in every note. And when that day comes, you will look back on these nights, these struggles, and know that every moment was worth it." His enthusiasm was infectious, a spark that reignited the fire within me, a reminder that my dreams, though distant, were within reach if I had the courage to pursue them.

With their encouragement in my heart, I returned to my work with renewed determination, each note a step forward, each melody a reflection of the journey that lay before me. And though my tools were limited, my spirit was not, for each song, each sound, was a reflection of the strength and hope that had sustained me, a reminder that even in the darkest of times, there is a light that cannot be extinguished.

But even as my dreams grew, so too did the challenges that lay before me. The path to creation was fraught with obstacles, each one a test of both skill and patience, a reminder that every achievement, every success, is built upon a foundation of struggle and sacrifice. And though I longed for more—for better tools, for the resources that might bring my vision to life—I knew that such things were not yet within my reach, that they would come only when the time was right.

In moments of frustration, when my laptop faltered or my melodies fell short of my vision, I would remember the words of my mother, her voice a steady anchor in the storms of my heart. "Allah tests those He loves," she would say, her gaze calm, her hands steady as she worked. "And through these tests, we grow, we learn, we become the people we are meant to be." Her words were a balm to my spirit, a reminder that my journey, though challenging, was blessed, a gift that I had been entrusted with, a gift that I was bound to honor.

And so, with each setback, I returned to my work, each note a reflection of my commitment, each melody a testament to the patience and resilience that my journey demanded. I experimented with new sounds, new techniques, pushing the limits of my humble equipment, seeking ways to bring my vision closer to reality. And though the process was slow, filled with moments of doubt and frustration, I found a peace in the act of creation, a joy that was both humbling and uplifting, a reminder that true success is measured not by what we achieve but by the heart with which we pursue our dreams.

One evening, as I sat before my laptop, a thought struck me—a vision of a song that might capture not only my own journey but the journey of all those who had walked beside me, who had shared in my struggles and my dreams. It would be a melody of resilience, a tribute to the strength and hope that had sustained us, a reminder that, even in the darkest of times, there is a light that cannot be extinguished.

The vision took hold of me, a melody that seemed to grow within my heart, a song that spoke of hope, of resilience, of the journey that had brought me to this point. It was a song that was both mine and not mine, a reflection of the people who had shaped my life, of the love and sacrifice that had guided me to this moment. And as I worked on this melody, I felt a sense of purpose that went beyond my own ambitions, a calling that transcended the boundaries of my own desires, a reminder that my journey was not for myself alone.

Yet, even as the song grew, so too did my desire for tools that could bring it to life in a way that did justice to its message. My laptop, though faithful, was limited, its sound distorted, its capabilities stretched to the very edge of what it could handle. I knew that if I were to bring this song to fruition, I would need more than what I had—I would need a microphone, a set of headphones, equipment that could capture the nuances, the subtleties, the emotions that my humble laptop could not convey.

But these tools were not within my reach. They were costly, luxuries in a life where every coin was carefully guarded, where each expense was weighed against the needs of survival. And so, I found myself at a crossroads, torn between the desire to bring my vision to life and the reality of my circumstances. It was a test, a trial that demanded both patience and faith, a reminder that even the purest dreams must sometimes wait for their time.

In the days that followed, I wrestled with this dilemma, my heart torn between ambition and restraint. I longed to create, to give voice to the melody that had taken hold of me, yet I knew that the path I sought was not one that could be forced, that every step forward required both sacrifice and wisdom. And so, I resolved to be patient, to continue working with what I had, trusting that in time, Allah would provide the means to bring my dreams to life.

And as I continued, I found within me a peace that I had not known before, a quiet assurance that my journey, though uncertain, was blessed. And though the tools I had were limited, my spirit was not, for each note, each song, was a reflection of the dreams that had taken root within me, dreams that spoke of hope, of resilience, of the strength that I had found within myself.

CHAPTER 3: FAITH AND PURPOSE

My journey in this world had been guided by dreams, yet it was a deeper calling that now stirred within me—a longing not just to achieve, but to understand, to seek the reason for my existence, to align my ambitions with the purpose granted by Allah. It began as a whisper in my soul, a voice that grew louder with each passing day, urging me to look beyond my own desires, to see my life not as a mere pursuit of success but as a means of serving a higher purpose.

With each dawn, as I took to my daily tasks, I found my mind turning to questions of faith, questions that sought answers not in the material world but in the spiritual, the eternal. What is the meaning of this life? What purpose does my Creator intend for me? And as these questions blossomed within me, I was compelled to turn to the teachings of Islam, to the words that held within them the wisdom of centuries, the guidance of Allah, my only source of truth.

I sought comfort in the pages of the Quran, in the verses that spoke of patience, resilience, and purpose. Each line seemed to reach into my heart, offering insights that resonated with the journey I was walking, reminding me that this life is but a test, a path toward something far greater than earthly rewards. And though I had only begun to grasp the depth of these teachings, I felt a pull toward a life that was not merely for my own gain but for the glory of Allah and the betterment of those around me.

Yet, as my faith deepened, so too did my struggle, for I found myself torn between the dreams that had shaped my life and the questions that now lingered in my heart. Could I, in good conscience, pursue a life in music, a path that, though filled with beauty, did not always align with the values that I held dear? Was my ambition a gift or a distraction, a calling or a temptation that might lead me astray from the path of righteousness?

Each day, as I practiced my music, as I poured my soul into each note, I felt the weight of this dilemma, a burden that grew heavier with each passing moment. For while I loved the art of creation, while I felt a purpose in the melodies that I crafted, I could not escape the feeling that this path might not be the one that Allah intended for me. And as I wrestled with these thoughts, I found myself turning once more to the Quran, seeking answers, guidance, and a sense of clarity.

In the stillness of the night, I would close my eyes and ask Allah for wisdom, for a sign that might reveal the truth of my path. And though the answers did not come swiftly, I felt a sense of peace, a quiet assurance that my journey, though filled with questions, was leading me closer to the truth, closer to a life that would honor both my Creator and the gifts He had bestowed upon me.

In my search for guidance, I found myself drawn to the words of the Quran, the passages that spoke of purpose, patience, and resilience. Each verse seemed to carry a message that was as ancient as it was relevant, a reminder that this life, though fleeting, holds within it a chance to prove ourselves, to rise above our desires and fulfill the purpose for which we were created. And as I read, I felt a sense of humility, a realization that my journey was not for myself alone but for Allah, for the honor of living a life that reflected His wisdom and mercy.

One verse in particular lingered within me, a verse that spoke of the fleeting nature of worldly pursuits, of the importance of seeking a life that is pleasing to Allah, a life rooted in faith and service. "Verily, with hardship comes ease," the words read, a reminder that every trial, every question, was a test, an opportunity to grow in strength and understanding. And as I pondered these words, I felt a renewed sense of purpose, a desire not merely to achieve but to serve, to live in a way that would honor both my family and my Creator.

Yet, even as I found comfort in these teachings, the struggle within me remained. For while I longed to follow the path of faith, I was still bound to the dreams that had shaped my life, dreams that spoke of music, of creation, of a calling that was both personal and profound. And as I wrestled with these conflicting desires, I knew that I could not make this decision alone, that I needed guidance, wisdom, and the strength to choose a path that would honor both my faith and my heart.

With a heart full of questions, I sought the counsel of my Imam, a man whose wisdom and faith had guided our community through countless trials, whose words held within them the strength of tradition and the depth of understanding. He listened patiently as I poured out my struggles, as I spoke of my love for music and my desire to honor Allah, of the conflict that had taken root within me, a conflict that I could not resolve on my own.

The Imam, his gaze steady and compassionate, offered words that were as gentle as they were profound. "My son," he said, his voice soft yet firm, "Allah has given each of us a gift, a talent that we are meant to use not for our own glory but for His. Wealth, when earned in a manner that is halal, is a blessing, a means by which we can support our families, help those in need, and bring honor to our faith. But remember, true wealth is not measured by riches alone, but by the goodness of one's heart, by the legacy one leaves behind."

His words struck a chord within me, a reminder that my journey was not merely about achievement but about purpose, about the way in which I chose to live, the values that guided my path. He spoke of the importance of halal wealth, of earning in a way that is pure, that is aligned with the teachings of Islam, a way that brings both honor and peace. And as I listened, I felt a sense of clarity, a realization that my journey was not defined by the path I chose but by the heart with which I walked it.

Yet, even as I absorbed the wisdom of my Imam, the questions within me remained. For while I understood the importance of earning in a way that was halal, I still found myself torn between the dreams that had shaped my life and the values that had been instilled within me. Was my music a calling or a temptation, a gift or a distraction? And as I wrestled with these thoughts, I found myself turning once more to the teachings of Islam, seeking answers that would help me find a path that was both true to my heart and aligned with my faith.

In the quiet of the night, as I pondered these questions, I felt a sense of humility, a realization that my journey was not merely for myself but for Allah, for the honor of living a life that reflected His wisdom and mercy. And though I did not yet have the answers, I felt a quiet confidence that, with patience and prayer, the truth would reveal itself, that Allah would guide me to a path that would honor both my faith and my dreams.

With each passing day, I grew more aware of the delicate balance that my journey required, a balance between ambition and humility, between faith and desire. And though the path was uncertain, I felt a quiet strength, a knowledge that my journey was guided by a wisdom far greater than my own, a wisdom that would lead me to the life I was meant to live, a life that would honor both my family and my Creator.

In my search for answers, I found myself turning to prayer, to the quiet moments in which I could lay my heart before Allah, seeking guidance, strength, and understanding. Each morning, as the sun rose over the village, I would rise and offer my prayers, my heart filled with both humility and hope, a hope that my Creator would grant me the wisdom to choose a path that would honor Him, a path that would bring peace to my soul and purpose to my life.

As I made a habit of daily prayer, I found within me a sense of peace, a quiet assurance that my journey, though filled with questions, was leading me closer to the truth. For in each prayer, I felt a connection to Allah, a reminder that my life was not for myself alone but for Him, for the honor of serving a purpose that was greater than my own desires. And though I did not yet know where this path would lead, I trusted that, with each step, I was drawing closer to a life that would reflect the values that had been instilled within me, values of faith, humility, and resilience.

In the stillness of these moments, I felt a strength that was not my own, a strength that came from the knowledge that my journey was guided by a wisdom far greater than my own. And as I continued to seek answers, I felt a quiet confidence that, with patience and faith, Allah would reveal the path that was meant for me, a path that would honor both my dreams and my duty to Him.

In my quest for purpose, I was drawn to a deeper understanding of wealth as it is viewed within Islam, a concept that went beyond mere material riches, beyond the shallow pursuit of status. My heart began to absorb a truth that was as ancient as it was profound—a truth that wealth, when earned through halal means and used wisely, was a blessing, a tool to uplift oneself and others, a means of serving Allah and supporting the community. In this understanding, wealth was not an end in itself, but a responsibility, a trust that came with both blessings and obligations.

As I contemplated this concept, I found myself humbled, for it reminded me that my ambitions were not merely for myself alone. They were a means by which I could serve others, a path that could lead not only to personal fulfillment but to the betterment of those around me. My father, who labored day and night in a foreign land, had not pursued wealth for its own sake but had done so with a heart full of purpose, a heart dedicated to supporting his family, to lifting us from the hardships that had defined our lives.

In this realization, I felt a renewed sense of purpose, a determination not only to achieve but to contribute, to live in a way that would honor both my family and my faith. And as I pondered the teachings of Islam, I felt a quiet resolve growing within me, a commitment to use whatever blessings I might receive in a way that was just and righteous, a way that would reflect the values that had been instilled within me since childhood.

Yet, even as my understanding deepened, the struggle within me remained. For while I had come to see wealth as a blessing, a means of service, I still wrestled with the question of music, a passion that seemed at once both noble and uncertain. Could I, in good conscience, pursue a career in music, a field that did not always align with the values of Islam? Was my love for this art a gift from Allah or a temptation that might lead me astray? These questions weighed heavily upon me, casting a shadow over my every note, my every melody.

There were days when doubt filled my heart, when I questioned not only my path but the purpose of my talents, wondering if they were a distraction rather than a calling. I knew that music held a power, a beauty that could touch the soul, yet I was uncertain if it was a path that could lead me closer to Allah or one that would pull me away from Him. In these moments, I found myself returning to the Quran, seeking answers, clarity, and a sense of peace.

The verses I read spoke of patience, of resilience, of the importance of living a life that is pleasing to Allah, a life that reflects the values of faith, humility, and service. And though these teachings did not offer a direct answer to my questions, they reminded me that my journey was one of growth, of learning, of finding a balance between my dreams and my duty to Allah. And as I pondered these words, I felt a quiet strength, a knowledge that, with patience and faith, the answers would reveal themselves in time.

Then came a moment I had long awaited—a moment when my music, humble and unpolished though it was, brought forth its first fruits. I had shared a piece online, a simple melody that reflected the journey of my soul, a tune that spoke of resilience, of faith, of the path I was walking. It was a song that held within it the strength of my spirit, a song that was both mine and not mine, a reflection of the journey that had brought me to this point.

And then, one day, I received a notification—a modest sum, a small payment for the music I had shared, a recognition, however humble, of the work I had poured into my art. My heart leapt with joy, a thrill of achievement, a sense that, perhaps, my dreams were not as distant as they seemed. Yet, as quickly as this joy filled my heart, it was joined by a sense of unease, a quiet guilt that lingered at the edges of my mind, a reminder that my journey was not merely about achievement but about purpose, about finding a path that honored both my faith and my ambitions.

In the quiet of that moment, I felt a mix of emotions—gratitude for the blessing, guilt for the doubts that still lingered, and a renewed determination to seek clarity, to find a path that would honor Allah, that would allow me to pursue my dreams with a heart that was both bold and humble. And as I pondered these feelings, I felt a quiet assurance that my journey, though uncertain, was blessed, that each step, each lesson, was leading me closer to the truth, closer to a life that would reflect both my faith and my dreams.

In my search for balance, I found myself drawn to prayer, to the moments of stillness in which I could lay my heart before Allah, seeking guidance, strength, and understanding. Each morning, as the sun rose over the village, I would rise and offer my prayers, my heart filled with both humility and hope, a hope that my Creator would grant me the wisdom to choose a path that would honor Him, a path that would bring peace to my soul and purpose to my life.

As I made a habit of daily prayer, I found within me a sense of peace, a quiet assurance that my journey, though filled with questions, was leading me closer to the truth. For in each prayer, I felt a connection to Allah, a reminder that my life was not for myself alone but for Him, for the honor of serving a purpose that was greater than my own desires. And though I did not yet know where this path would lead, I trusted that, with each step, I was drawing closer to a life that would reflect the values that had been instilled within me, values of faith, humility, and resilience.

In the stillness of these moments, I felt a strength that was not my own, a strength that came from the knowledge that my journey was guided by a wisdom far greater than my own. And as I continued to seek answers, I felt a quiet confidence that, with patience and faith, Allah would reveal the path that was meant for me, a path that would honor both my dreams and my duty to Him.

Then, one evening, as I pondered these questions in the solitude of my room, my father's words came to me, a reminder of the values he had instilled in me, values of honor, humility, and faith. He, who had sacrificed so much to provide for us, had walked a path that was guided not by ambition but by duty, by a love that was as selfless as it was profound. And as I thought of his journey, I felt a renewed sense of purpose, a desire not only to achieve but to make choices that would honor his sacrifice, that would reflect the values he had taught me.

The following morning, I sought him out, my heart filled with questions, my mind filled with doubts. He listened as I spoke of my love for music, of the struggle within me, the desire to pursue a life that would honor both my dreams and my faith. His face, though lined with years of labor, softened as he listened, his eyes filled with a compassion that brought tears to my own.

"Afjal," he said, his voice steady, "in this life, we are given a choice, a chance to walk a path that will bring honor not only to ourselves but to those who have come before us, to those who will come after. Wealth, success—these are gifts, blessings that we must use wisely, for they are but a trust from Allah, a chance to make a difference, to lift others, to honor the values that have shaped us. Walk the path that speaks to your soul, but walk it with a heart that is true, a heart that honors both your family and your faith."

His words, though simple, struck a chord within me, a reminder that my journey was not merely about achievement but about purpose, about living a life that would reflect the values that had been instilled within me since childhood. And as I looked into his eyes, I felt a sense of peace, a knowledge that my path, though uncertain, was one that I could walk with pride, one that would honor both my family and my faith.

In my search for direction, I sought out voices of wisdom—those who had walked this path before me, Muslims who had built lives of purpose and integrity while staying true to their faith. I found inspiration in their stories, tales of perseverance, of faith that did not falter even in the face of hardship. These mentors, though I knew them not in person, became guiding lights, examples of how a person could live a life of honor, could seek success in a way that was halal, that brought blessings not only upon themselves but upon others.

Their stories reminded me that success, in its truest form, is not measured by wealth or fame but by the impact one has upon the lives of others, by the goodness that one brings into the world. I read of men and women who had dedicated their wealth to causes of justice, to the care of orphans, to the spread of knowledge, their actions a testament to the power of faith when it is wielded with humility and compassion. And in their lives, I found a model, a way to pursue my own dreams in a manner that was both ambitious and righteous, a path that would honor both my family and my Creator.

Yet, even as I absorbed these lessons, I knew that my journey was unique, that my path would require me to make choices that reflected my own heart, my own faith. And as I pondered the lives of these mentors, I felt a sense of purpose growing within me, a desire not only to achieve but to contribute, to use my talents in a way that would bring honor not only to myself but to the community that had shaped me, to the family that had sacrificed so much for me.

As I continued on this path, I began to understand the importance of gratitude, a virtue that had been instilled in me since childhood yet had taken on new meaning as I walked this journey of self-discovery. Each small success, each step forward, was a reminder of the blessings that Allah had granted me, of the opportunities that I had been given, opportunities that others might never see. And as I reflected upon these blessings, I felt a sense of humility, a realization that my journey, though difficult, was a gift, a chance to prove myself, to use my talents in a way that would reflect the values that had shaped me.

In moments of frustration, when my progress seemed slow, when the challenges seemed insurmountable, I would remind myself of the blessings that had brought me to this point, of the family who had supported me, of the friends who had believed in me even when I struggled to believe in myself. And in this gratitude, I found a strength, a resilience that could not be shaken, for it reminded me that my journey was not mine alone, that it was a testament to the sacrifices of those who had come before me, a continuation of the legacy that my father and mother had built with their own hands.

With each success, however small, I would pause to offer a prayer of thanks, a reminder that my journey was guided not by my own strength but by the blessings of Allah. And as I practiced this gratitude, I found a peace, a joy that came not from achievement alone but from the knowledge that I was walking a path that was both humble and righteous, a path that honored both my family and my faith.

As my understanding deepened, I found myself considering new paths, alternatives that might align more closely with my values, with the principles that had been instilled within me since childhood. Music, though a passion, was a path filled with uncertainty, a path that did not always align with the teachings of Islam, with the values of humility and service that had shaped my life. And as I pondered these questions, I felt a quiet urge to explore other avenues, paths that might offer a way to serve others while still pursuing my dreams.

I began to research new fields, industries where I might use my creativity, my drive, in a way that was both ambitious and halal. Marketing, technology, business—these were fields where I might find a way to contribute, to build a career that was both successful and honorable, a career that would allow me to support my family, to give back to my community, to live a life that reflected the values of Islam. And though these paths were unfamiliar, they held within them a promise, a chance to walk a path that was both righteous and fulfilling.

In these moments of exploration, I felt a sense of excitement, a reminder that my journey was not limited by my past but was shaped by my choices, by the decisions I made in each moment, decisions that could lead me to a life of purpose, a life that would bring honor to my family and glory to Allah. And as I considered these possibilities, I felt a renewed sense of hope, a quiet assurance that, with faith and perseverance, I could build a life that was both successful and honorable, a life that would reflect the values that had been instilled within me since childhood.

With each passing day, I grew more committed to my faith, more determined to walk a path that would honor Allah, that would bring peace to my soul and purpose to my life. My journey, though uncertain, was filled with lessons, lessons that reminded me of the importance of integrity, of the need to stay true to the values that had shaped my life, values of humility, of compassion, of faith. And as I continued on this path, I felt a sense of clarity, a knowledge that my purpose was not to achieve for myself alone but to contribute, to use my talents in a way that would serve others, that would reflect the goodness of Allah.

Each morning, as I offered my prayers, I felt a connection to my Creator, a reminder that my journey was not mine alone, that it was guided by a wisdom far greater than my own. And in these moments of prayer, I found a strength, a resilience that carried me through even the darkest of times, a reminder that my life was a gift, a chance to serve, to honor the blessings that had been bestowed upon me.

In my heart, I made a vow, a promise to walk this path with integrity, to stay true to the values that had shaped me, no matter where my journey might lead. For in this commitment, I found a peace, a joy that came not from achievement alone but from the knowledge that I was walking a path that was both humble and righteous, a path that honored both my faith and my family.

With this newfound clarity, I continued my journey, each step a reflection of the purpose that had taken root within me, a purpose that was both personal and profound, a purpose that would guide me through the challenges that lay ahead, challenges that I was determined to face with a heart that was both bold and humble, a heart that honored both my dreams and my duty to Allah.

And then, one evening, as I sat in the quiet solitude of my room, the decision that I had long avoided came to me, a decision that was both difficult and liberating. I knew, in my heart, that I could not continue on this path of music, that my dreams, though beautiful, did not align with the values that had shaped my life, with the teachings of Islam. It was a realization that filled me with both sorrow and peace, a reminder that my journey, though uncertain, was guided by a wisdom far greater than my own.

In this moment of clarity, I felt a sense of peace, a knowledge that my journey was not for myself alone but for Allah, for the honor of living a life that would reflect His wisdom and mercy. And though the decision to leave music was painful, I felt a quiet assurance that my path, though challenging, was blessed, that each step, each lesson, was leading me closer to the truth, closer to a life that would reflect both my faith and my dreams.

With a heart full of gratitude, I offered a prayer of thanks, a reminder that my journey was guided not by my own strength but by the blessings of Allah. And as I embraced this decision, I felt a peace that could not be shaken, a peace that came not from achievement alone but from the knowledge that I was walking a path that was both humble and righteous, a path that honored both my family and my faith.

As I closed this chapter of my life, I felt a sense of freedom, a sense of purpose that went beyond my own ambitions. I knew that my journey was just beginning, that there were paths yet to be discovered, dreams yet to be fulfilled, dreams that would align with my faith, that would bring peace to my soul and purpose to my life. And as I looked to the future, I felt a quiet confidence, a knowledge that, with faith and perseverance, I could build a life that would honor both my family and my Creator.

With each step forward, I felt a sense of purpose, a determination to pursue a life that was both righteous and fulfilling, a life that would reflect the values that had shaped me, values of humility, of compassion, of faith. And though my journey was uncertain, I trusted that Allah would guide me, that

He would lead me to a path that was both successful and honorable, a path that would bring honor to my family and glory to Him.

With a heart full of faith, I stepped forward, trusting that my journey, though filled with questions, was leading me closer to the truth, closer to a life that would reflect both my faith and my dreams.

CHAPTER 4: FACING REALITY

With the decision to leave music, a strange mixture of emotions settled over me—part relief, part sorrow, a quiet sense of uncertainty that both liberated and unsettled my soul. I had closed the door on a chapter that had once defined me, a chapter that had offered a glimpse of my dreams, a taste of the creative joy that had carried me through moments of struggle. Yet, as I looked upon the road that stretched before me, I found myself questioning this choice, wondering if I had surrendered too hastily, if I had let go of a gift that had brought me so close to my heart's desires.

The quiet solitude of the night became my sanctuary, a time to ponder my choices, to sift through the doubts that lingered in the corners of my mind. Had I truly abandoned this path out of devotion, or had fear played a part, fear of a journey that might lead me astray from my faith? The question weighed heavily upon me, and as I searched for answers, I felt a sense of peace that came not from understanding, but from a faith that assured me I was not alone, that my journey, though uncertain, was guided by a wisdom beyond my own.

In those moments of reflection, I reminded myself of the purpose that had driven my choice—the desire to live a life that honored Allah, a life that would bring not only success but meaning, a sense of fulfillment that went beyond mere ambition. And though the road ahead was unclear, I felt a quiet confidence that, with patience and faith, I would find my way, that Allah would reveal a path that would align with both my dreams and my devotion.

The days that followed were marked by a sense of loss, a feeling of displacement that left me adrift, unsure of where I belonged or what lay ahead. The dreams I had once held with such certainty now seemed distant, mere echoes of a life that I could no longer call my own. And as I navigated this new reality, I found myself grappling with doubts, with questions that had no easy answers, with a fear that perhaps I had abandoned my one true calling, that I had surrendered to the pressures of uncertainty rather than the clarity of purpose.

In these moments, regret lingered at the edges of my mind, a reminder of the path I had chosen to forsake, a path that had offered a glimpse of possibility, a sense of identity that now felt fragmented, incomplete. I would gaze at the instrument that once held my dreams, feeling the weight of decisions that had been made with conviction, yet now seemed shadowed by a sense of loss. Had I acted too hastily, surrendering a gift that had brought me joy, a gift that had defined my journey for so long?

And yet, beneath the sorrow and doubt, I felt a quiet resolve, a determination to press forward, to find a new path that would bring peace to my soul and purpose to my life. I reminded myself of the commitment I had made, the vow to pursue a life that would honor Allah, a life that would bring blessings not only upon myself but upon those around me. And though the future was uncertain, I resolved to trust in the guidance of my Creator, to believe that every choice, every moment, was leading me closer to the life I was meant to live.

With a heart full of questions, I began to explore new possibilities, paths that might align with my values, with the principles that had been instilled within me since childhood. The world was vast, filled with opportunities that I had yet to discover, and as I looked upon these choices, I felt a spark of curiosity, a desire to find a way to contribute, to build a life that was both meaningful and honorable. I knew that my journey would require patience, that I would need to approach each path with a heart both open and discerning, a heart that sought not only success but a purpose that resonated with my faith.

As I considered these new paths, I felt a quiet thrill, a sense of excitement that reminded me that my life was not limited by my past but was shaped by the choices I made in each moment. Perhaps I would find a way to use my creativity in a manner that aligned with my values, a way to pursue my ambitions in a way that was both halal and fulfilling. And though I did not yet know where this journey would lead, I felt a renewed sense of hope, a belief that Allah would guide me to a path that would bring both joy and purpose.

In the solitude of these reflections, I found a sense of peace, a reminder that my life was not defined by the choices I had made but by the heart with which I walked this path, by the faith that carried me through each moment of uncertainty. And as I pondered these new possibilities, I resolved to approach each step with humility, to trust that, with patience and faith, I would find a way to honor both my family and my Creator.

One evening, as I delved into my search for a new path, I came across the concept of online business, a world of digital commerce that was as vast as it was intriguing. Dropshipping, digital marketing—these were terms that had once held little meaning to me, yet now seemed to hold a promise, a potential path that might allow me to build a life that was both successful and aligned with my faith. The idea of running a business from my own home, of creating something that could bring both profit and purpose, filled me with a sense of possibility, a belief that perhaps this was the way forward.

I began to study the basics, to learn about the world of online commerce, to understand the mechanics of dropshipping, a business model that required neither inventory nor a physical storefront, only a connection to the vast marketplace of the internet. It was a concept that seemed almost too good to be true, a way to generate income without the need for large investments or extensive resources. And as I explored this new field, I felt a spark of ambition, a desire to create something that would bring both success and stability, a path that could support not only myself but my family.

Yet, even as I embraced this new path, I felt a sense of caution, a reminder that true success requires both effort and integrity, that wealth, when earned in a manner that is halal, brings not only blessings but responsibility. And as I prepared to embark upon this journey, I resolved to approach it with a heart that was both diligent and discerning, to ensure that my efforts were rooted not only in ambition but in a desire to serve, to contribute, to build a life that would bring honor to Allah and to those who had sacrificed for my success.

As I delved deeper into the world of online business, I quickly discovered that the path was not as simple as it had seemed. Dropshipping, though promising in theory, required skills and resources that I had yet to acquire—a knowledge of digital marketing, an understanding of supply chains, a sense of business strategy that could turn potential into profit. And as I confronted these challenges, I found myself facing the reality of this journey, a reality that demanded not only ambition but a willingness to learn, to grow, to adapt.

The world of digital commerce was vast, a marketplace filled with competition, with businesses that had established their presence long before I had entered the field. And as I navigated this new reality, I felt a sense of both excitement and trepidation, a realization that this journey would require both perseverance and patience, a commitment to learning the skills that would allow me to succeed in a world that was as dynamic as it was demanding.

Yet, even as I faced these challenges, I felt a quiet resolve, a determination to overcome the obstacles that lay before me, to build a foundation that would support not only my ambitions but my values. And though the path was uncertain, I resolved to approach each challenge with humility, to trust that, with patience and effort, I could find a way to build a business that was both successful and halal, a business that would bring both profit and purpose, a business that would honor both my family and my faith.

The first steps into this new world of digital commerce revealed layers of complexity that I had not anticipated. Each article I read, each tutorial I studied, opened my eyes to a world that was as demanding as it was promising. Dropshipping was no mere venture; it required strategy, planning, and a patience that I was only beginning to cultivate. Success in this field, I realized, was not granted swiftly, nor without a commitment to learning and adapting to the constantly changing landscape of online business.

My days became a blend of research and practice, hours spent learning about supply chains, studying digital marketing techniques, understanding customer psychology, and the art of building a brand that would resonate with potential buyers. It was a journey that required not only technical skill but a vision, a belief in the product I would eventually offer, a sense of purpose that went beyond profit. For while wealth was a part of this journey, I knew that true success would require a commitment to quality, a dedication to serving my customers with honesty and integrity.

Yet, even as I immersed myself in this new field, doubts lingered. Could I, with my limited resources and humble beginnings, build a business that would stand out in a marketplace filled with seasoned entrepreneurs and established brands? The thought weighed upon me, a quiet reminder of the challenges that lay before me, challenges that demanded not only ambition but resilience, a willingness to continue even when the odds seemed stacked against me.

In these moments of doubt, I found myself turning once again to my faith, to the teachings of Islam that spoke of patience, of resilience, of the importance of trusting in Allah's plan. For though I could not yet see the path before me clearly, I believed that each challenge, each setback, was a test, a chance to prove my dedication, my commitment to building a life that was both successful and righteous. And as I pondered these teachings, I felt a renewed sense of purpose, a quiet assurance that, with patience and effort, I could build a business that would bring both profit and purpose, a business that would honor both my family and my Creator.

As I continued my research, I came across a topic that struck a chord within me—the concept of branding, the art of creating an identity for a business, an image that would resonate with customers and leave a lasting impression. It was a concept that went beyond mere products; it was about building a story, a narrative that connected with people on a deeper level, a sense of purpose that would make the brand memorable, meaningful. And as I pondered this idea, I felt a spark of inspiration, a realization that branding could be more than a business strategy—it could be a reflection of the values that had shaped my life.

My brand, I decided, would be more than a marketplace; it would be a platform that reflected my journey, my commitment to honesty, quality, and service. I would build a business that was not merely about profit but about providing value, about offering products that could benefit people, products that were halal, ethical, and sourced with care. And in this vision, I found a sense of purpose, a belief that my business could be a means of serving others, a way to bring goodness into the world, to honor Allah through the work of my hands.

Yet, as I embraced this vision, I knew that the path would not be easy. Branding required resources, an investment of both time and money, a commitment to building a foundation that could support this vision, a foundation that could withstand the challenges that would inevitably come. And though I was prepared to make these sacrifices, I felt a sense of trepidation, a fear that perhaps my vision was too ambitious, that I was reaching beyond my means, beyond the limits of what was possible for someone with my background and resources.

But even in the face of these doubts, I resolved to move forward, to trust in the vision that had taken root within me, to believe that Allah, in His wisdom, would guide my steps, that He would provide the strength and resources needed to turn this dream into reality. And as I took each step, I reminded myself of the values that had guided me, the principles of integrity and humility, of resilience and patience, principles that I would carry with me through each challenge, each decision, each moment of this journey.

In the early days of my business, I faced a series of obstacles that tested my resolve, challenges that forced me to confront the realities of this new path, to adapt, to learn, and to persevere. The first of these challenges was the issue of sourcing products, a task that seemed simple in theory yet proved far more complex in practice. Finding suppliers who met my standards, who offered products that were both quality and halal, was no easy feat, a task that required both patience and diligence, a commitment to upholding the values that had guided me since childhood.

Each day became a cycle of research and negotiation, hours spent comparing suppliers, analyzing quality, calculating costs, and assessing the reliability of each option. And as I navigated this process, I found myself facing moments of frustration, moments when it seemed that every supplier fell short of the standards I had set, that every option required a compromise, a sacrifice that I was unwilling to make. Yet, even in these moments of frustration, I reminded myself of the commitment I had made, the promise to build a business that was both profitable and honorable, a business that would reflect the values that had shaped my life.

In the end, I found a supplier who met my standards, a company that shared my commitment to quality, to ethical sourcing, to the principles of halal commerce. And as I signed the contract, I felt a sense of accomplishment, a reminder that every challenge, every moment of patience, was leading me closer to the vision I held, a vision that was both personal and profound, a vision that would bring both success and purpose, a vision that would honor both my family and my faith.

This first step, though small, marked the beginning of my journey, a journey that would be filled with challenges and triumphs, with moments of doubt and moments of clarity, a journey that would test not only my skills but my character, my resilience, my faith. And as I took each step forward, I resolved to approach each challenge with a heart that was both bold and humble, a heart that trusted in Allah's guidance, a heart that believed in the goodness of this path.

With the foundation of my business in place, I turned my attention to the next phase of the journey—the creation of an online store, a platform where my brand could come to life, a space where I could connect with customers, share my vision, and offer products that were both meaningful and valuable. Building an online store was a task that demanded both technical skill and creative vision, a combination of strategy and artistry, a blend of functionality and aesthetics that would make the website both accessible and engaging.

As I began this process, I quickly discovered that creating an online store was no simple task. Each detail, from the design of the homepage to the layout of the product pages, required careful consideration, a commitment to creating a space that was both inviting and professional. I spent hours studying the websites of successful brands, analyzing their designs, learning from their strategies, seeking inspiration that could guide me as I crafted my own store. And in each detail, I felt a sense of purpose, a belief that my work was not merely about selling products but about creating a platform that reflected my journey, my values, my vision.

The process was both challenging and exhilarating, a journey of discovery that allowed me to bring my creativity to life, to shape a space that was both functional and inspiring, a space that would resonate with customers and offer them an experience that was both valuable and authentic. And as I worked, I felt a sense of pride, a knowledge that I was building something that was both meaningful and honorable, a business that would reflect the principles that had guided me, a business that would bring both profit and purpose.

Yet, even as I embraced this journey, I knew that the road ahead was filled with challenges, that building a successful online store was only the first step, that true success would require a commitment to growth, a willingness to adapt, to learn, to persevere. And as I prepared for the challenges that lay ahead, I resolved to approach each step with humility, to trust that, with patience and faith, I could build a business that would bring both blessings and success, a business that would honor both my family and my faith.

As I poured my efforts into creating the online store, I encountered a new challenge that tested my patience and resourcefulness—marketing. I had read of its importance, of how crucial it was to reach the right audience, to share my brand's vision in a way that would resonate with potential customers. Yet, as I delved deeper, I realized that marketing was an art, a delicate balance of strategy and creativity, a process that required a profound understanding of human nature, of what draws people in, what captures their interest, what inspires trust.

Each day became a cycle of experimentation and learning, of trial and error, as I explored different methods—social media ads, content creation, email campaigns. I studied the techniques of successful brands, analyzing their methods, learning from their successes and failures, seeking insights that could guide my own strategy. But each step felt like an uphill battle, each technique a new language I had to learn, a new skill I had to master, and the journey was often frustrating, filled with moments of doubt and uncertainty.

Yet, even in these challenges, I found a sense of purpose, a reminder that my journey was not merely about profit but about growth, about developing skills that would serve me in every aspect of life, about building resilience and learning to adapt. Marketing, I realized, was not just a tool for business—it was a way to connect, to share my story, to bring my vision to life in a way that would resonate with others, a way to create a brand that was not just a marketplace but a message, a reflection of my values.

And though the road was long, I resolved to embrace each challenge with humility, to trust that every obstacle, every moment of frustration, was a stepping stone, a chance to grow, to learn, to become the person I was meant to be. For in each challenge, I saw an opportunity, a reminder that my journey was guided by a wisdom far greater than my own, a wisdom that was leading me toward a life that would honor both my family and my faith.

In the midst of these efforts, I encountered the power of feedback, a lesson that was both humbling and enlightening. As my online store began to gain traction, as customers began to visit, I received my first reviews, my first comments from those who had purchased my products, who had interacted with my brand. Some of the feedback was positive, words of encouragement that filled my heart with a sense of pride, a reminder that my work was making a difference, that my vision was resonating with others.

Yet, not all feedback was favorable. Some customers pointed out flaws, areas where my products fell short of expectations, aspects of the website that could be improved, details that I had overlooked in my haste to bring my brand to life. At first, these critiques felt like a blow, a reminder of my own inexperience, my own limitations, a challenge to the vision I held so dearly. But as I pondered these comments, I realized that feedback, though often difficult to hear, was a gift, an opportunity to grow, to refine my work, to build a business that was truly valuable, truly aligned with my values.

With each piece of feedback, I found myself re-evaluating, seeking ways to improve, to address the concerns of my customers with a heart that was both humble and committed. And as I embraced this process, I felt a sense of growth, a knowledge that my journey, though filled with challenges, was leading me toward a life that was both successful and honorable, a life that would reflect the values that had guided me since childhood. For in each critique, I saw an opportunity, a chance to refine my vision, to build a business that would bring both profit and purpose, a business that would honor both my family and my faith.

With each day, as I continued to build and refine my business, I found myself facing a question that was as challenging as it was profound—the question of growth. For while my store had begun as a humble endeavor, a small venture that reflected my values, it was beginning to grow, to attract a larger audience, to demand more time, more resources, more commitment. And as this growth unfolded, I found myself wondering if I was prepared to handle the responsibilities that came with it, if I was ready to scale my business in a way that was both sustainable and ethical.

Growth, I realized, was not merely about profit; it was about impact, about the responsibility to serve my customers with integrity, to build a brand that would remain true to its values even as it expanded. And as I pondered these responsibilities, I felt a mixture of excitement and trepidation, a reminder that success, when pursued with integrity, comes with obligations, with a duty to uphold the standards that had guided me since the beginning.

Each decision, each step forward, became a test, a chance to prove my commitment to the values that had shaped my life, a reminder that my journey was not merely about achievement but about service, about building a brand that would bring honor not only to myself but to Allah. And though the road was filled with challenges, I resolved to approach each step with a heart that was both humble and ambitious, a heart that trusted in the guidance of Allah, a heart that believed in the goodness of this path.

In these moments, I found myself returning once more to the teachings of Islam, to the principles of honesty, humility, and compassion, principles that reminded me that true success is not measured by wealth alone but by the impact one has upon the lives of others. And as I embraced these teachings, I felt a renewed sense of purpose, a commitment to build a business that was not merely profitable but meaningful, a business that would reflect the values that had guided me, a business that would bring both blessings and success.

The journey of building this business became not only a path of learning and growth but a test of faith, a reminder that true resilience comes not from one's own strength but from the strength granted by Allah. Each challenge, each obstacle, became a lesson in patience, a chance to prove my dedication to the vision I held, a vision that was both ambitious and righteous, a vision that would bring honor not only to myself but to the community that had shaped me.

One evening, as I reflected upon this journey, I found myself pondering the nature of success, wondering if I had truly understood its meaning. For while I had long believed that success was measured by wealth, by achievement, by the accolades of others, I now saw that true success was far deeper, far more profound. Success, I realized, was not a destination but a journey, a path that required both humility and resilience, a commitment to living a life that was both righteous and honorable.

In these moments of reflection, I felt a sense of peace, a quiet assurance that my journey, though challenging, was leading me closer to the truth, closer to a life that would reflect the values that had been instilled within me since childhood. And as I continued on this path, I resolved to trust in Allah, to believe that every challenge, every obstacle, was a test, a chance to grow, to learn, to become the person I was meant to be.

For in each moment of doubt, in each moment of struggle, I found a strength that was not my own, a resilience that came from the knowledge that my journey was guided by a wisdom far greater than my own. And as I embraced this strength, I felt a renewed sense of purpose, a commitment to build a life that would bring both success and honor, a life that would reflect the goodness of Allah and the values that had shaped me.

With each step forward, my journey in business became a mirror, reflecting back at me the depth of my character, my resilience, and the values that had shaped me. I learned that success, though desirable, was not a single moment of achievement but a series of choices, each one a test of my commitment to the principles I held dear. As my brand began to gain visibility, as orders began to increase, I faced a new challenge—the demand to keep pace, to meet the expectations of my customers, to deliver not just products but a service that reflected the values of honesty, integrity, and care.

The process of fulfilling orders, of managing inventory, of coordinating with suppliers became a routine that was as demanding as it was rewarding.

Each order was a small victory, a reminder that my work was reaching people, that my vision was resonating, that my efforts were bearing fruit. Yet, with this growth came a responsibility, a duty to ensure that each product, each interaction, was aligned with the standards I had set, a commitment to quality that I refused to compromise, even in moments of pressure and exhaustion.

There were nights when I worked late into the evening, my hands weary, my eyes strained, yet my heart filled with a quiet pride, a sense that I was building something meaningful, something that would bring honor to my family and to Allah. In those quiet hours, I found a sense of purpose that went beyond profit, a joy that came not from wealth but from the knowledge that I was serving others, that I was creating a brand that reflected the goodness I had been taught, a brand that was rooted in the values of my faith.

And though the journey was challenging, I resolved to approach each step with humility, to remember that my business was not for myself alone but for the benefit of others, a means of providing value, of offering products that were halal, ethical, and meaningful. For in each order, I saw an opportunity to serve, a chance to build a legacy that would bring blessings not only upon myself but upon those who had supported me, those who had believed in me, those who had guided me toward this path.

As my business continued to grow, I encountered a lesson that was both humbling and enlightening—the lesson of humility, the realization that true success requires a heart that is both bold and humble, a heart that seeks not only to achieve but to uplift others. In moments of success, it is easy to lose oneself, to be swept away by the thrill of accomplishment, to forget the purpose that had once guided each step. Yet, as I navigated this journey, I found myself grounded by the teachings of Islam, teachings that reminded me that wealth and success, when pursued without humility, become hollow, mere shadows of true achievement.

Each success, each milestone, became a reminder of the blessings that Allah had granted me, a reminder that my journey, though filled with challenges, was a gift, an opportunity to prove myself, to use my talents in a way that would reflect the values that had shaped my life. And as I embraced this humility, I felt a sense of peace, a knowledge that my journey was guided not by my own strength but by the blessings of Allah, blessings that were both a gift and a responsibility, a chance to serve others, to honor the legacy of my family, to build a business that was both successful and righteous.

In moments of doubt, I would turn to prayer, seeking guidance, strength, and understanding, a reminder that my journey was not mine alone but a path that had been set for me, a journey that required both resilience and humility, a journey that would bring both success and honor, a journey that would reflect the goodness of Allah. And in each prayer, I found a strength that was not my own, a resilience that carried me through even the darkest of times, a reminder that my life was a gift, a chance to serve, to honor the blessings that had been bestowed upon me.

One of the most significant challenges I encountered was the need to balance my ambitions with the principles of fairness and honesty, a challenge that tested not only my business acumen but my character, my commitment to the values that had guided me since childhood. As orders grew and demand increased, I was faced with choices—choices that required me to balance profit with integrity, to ensure that each decision reflected not only my goals but my faith, a faith that demanded honesty, fairness, and compassion.

There were moments when I was tempted to take shortcuts, to sacrifice quality for speed, to increase prices without justification. Yet, in these moments, I felt a quiet voice within me, a reminder that true success is measured not by wealth alone but by the impact one has upon the lives of others, by the goodness that one brings into the world. And as I heeded this voice, I felt a sense of peace, a knowledge that my journey, though challenging, was guided by a wisdom far greater than my own, a wisdom that would lead me to a life that was both successful and honorable.

With each decision, I found myself returning to the teachings of Islam, to the principles of honesty and humility, to the values that had shaped my life, values that reminded me that wealth, when pursued without integrity, becomes hollow, a shadow of true success. And as I embraced these teachings, I felt a renewed sense of purpose, a commitment to build a business that was not merely profitable but meaningful, a business that would reflect the values that had guided me, a business that would bring both blessings and success.

In the end, I chose to build my brand with integrity, to prioritize quality over profit, to ensure that each product, each interaction, reflected the standards I had set, a commitment to honesty, fairness, and service. And though this path was challenging, I felt a quiet satisfaction, a knowledge that I was building a business that would honor both my family and my faith, a business that would bring both success and purpose, a business that would reflect the goodness of Allah.

In the midst of these efforts, I began to see the impact of my work, the way in which my brand was resonating with customers, the way in which my vision was taking shape, becoming a reality that was both rewarding and humbling. Each order, each review, was a reminder that my work was reaching people, that my efforts were making a difference, that my brand was becoming more than a business—it was becoming a community, a space where people could find products that were halal, ethical, and meaningful.

With each success, I felt a sense of pride, a knowledge that I was building something that was not only profitable but valuable, something that was not only successful but honorable, something that would bring both blessings and success. And as I embraced this journey, I felt a renewed sense of purpose, a commitment to continue, to build a legacy that would bring honor to my family, to serve others, to use my talents in a way that would reflect the values of Islam.

Yet, even in these moments of success, I remained mindful of the responsibility that came with it, a responsibility to serve my customers with integrity, to uphold the values that had guided me, to build a business that was both successful and righteous. For in each success, I saw a reminder that my journey was guided not by my own strength but by the blessings of Allah, blessings that were both a gift and a responsibility, a chance to serve, to honor the legacy of my family, to build a life that would bring both success and honor.

In these moments of reflection, I felt a sense of peace, a knowledge that my journey, though challenging, was leading me closer to the truth, closer to a life that would reflect the values that had been instilled within me since childhood. And as I continued on this path, I resolved to trust in Allah, to believe that every challenge, every obstacle, was a test, a chance to grow, to learn, to become the person I was meant to be.

As my journey in business continued, I found myself facing a new and unexpected challenge—the test of patience in the face of setbacks. In the world of online commerce, success is rarely linear; it is a path marked by fluctuations, by moments of triumph and moments of struggle, by days when everything seems to fall into place and others when each step feels like an uphill climb. There were times when orders slowed, when the carefully planned campaigns yielded little, when it seemed that every effort was met with silence, a stillness that tested my resolve, my faith in the path I had chosen.

In these moments of quiet, when results were slow to come, I found myself wrestling with doubt, wondering if my vision had been too ambitious, if my hopes had outpaced my resources, if my journey was destined to falter before it had truly begun. Yet, even as these doubts crept in, I felt a quiet reminder, a call to trust in the process, to believe that every journey has its seasons, that every endeavor requires both perseverance and faith, that success, when pursued with patience, becomes more than a fleeting victory— it becomes a testament to one's resilience.

Each day, I reminded myself of the teachings of Islam, the verses that spoke of patience, of resilience, of trusting in Allah's timing, a reminder that every setback, every delay, was a test, a chance to prove my dedication to the values that had shaped my life. And as I embraced these teachings, I found a renewed strength, a resilience that carried me through the moments of struggle, a belief that, with patience and perseverance, my efforts would bear fruit, that my journey, though challenging, was blessed.

In these quiet moments, I found a peace that went beyond results, a joy that came not from achievement alone but from the knowledge that I was building something meaningful, something that would bring both success and honor, something that would reflect the goodness of Allah and the values that had guided me since childhood. And though the road was long, I resolved to approach each challenge with humility, to trust that, with faith, every setback would become a stepping stone, a lesson that would lead me closer to the life I was meant to live.

With each challenge, I grew more aware of the importance of consistency, the quiet strength that comes from showing up each day, from taking small steps forward even when progress seems slow, even when results are hard to see. In the world of business, consistency is both a discipline and an art, a commitment to one's vision, a dedication to building something lasting, something that goes beyond the fleeting trends of the market. And as I embraced this discipline, I felt a sense of purpose, a belief that each effort, however small, was building a foundation, a legacy that would bring both profit and purpose.

Each morning, I would rise with a heart full of determination, a resolve to move forward, to take each step with a spirit of resilience, a belief that each effort, each task, was leading me closer to my vision, closer to a life that would reflect the values that had guided me since childhood. And though the journey was challenging, though the road was filled with obstacles, I felt a quiet strength, a resilience that carried me through each moment of doubt, a belief that my journey, though uncertain, was guided by a wisdom far greater than my own.

In moments of frustration, when the weight of my responsibilities seemed heavy, I found myself turning to prayer, seeking guidance, strength, and understanding, a reminder that my journey was not mine alone but a path that had been set for me, a journey that required both resilience and humility, a journey that would bring both success and honor, a journey that would reflect the goodness of Allah. And as I embraced this strength, I felt a renewed sense of purpose, a commitment to build a life that would bring both success and honor, a life that would reflect the values of Islam and the legacy of my family.

In the midst of this journey, I learned the value of reflection, the importance of pausing to consider one's progress, to evaluate each step, to ensure that every decision, every action, was aligned with the purpose that had guided me since the beginning. Reflection, I found, was not merely an act of self-evaluation; it was a way to stay grounded, a reminder that success, when pursued without humility, becomes a hollow victory, a shadow of true achievement. And as I embraced this practice, I felt a sense of peace, a reminder that my journey was not defined by results alone but by the heart with which I pursued it.

Each week, I would take a moment to consider my progress, to reflect upon the lessons I had learned, the challenges I had faced, the victories I had achieved, however small. In these moments, I found a sense of gratitude, a knowledge that my journey, though filled with challenges, was blessed, a gift that allowed me to grow, to learn, to become the person I was meant to be. For in each challenge, I saw an opportunity, a chance to refine my vision, to build a business that would bring both profit and purpose, a business that would honor both my family and my faith.

In these moments of reflection, I found myself returning once more to the teachings of Islam, to the principles of honesty, humility, and service, values that reminded me that true success is measured not by wealth alone but by the impact one has upon the lives of others. And as I embraced these teachings, I felt a renewed sense of purpose, a commitment to build a business that was not merely profitable but meaningful, a business that would reflect the values that had guided me, a business that would bring both blessings and success.

As the weeks turned into months, my business began to take on a life of its own, a rhythm that was both exhilarating and humbling. With each order, each interaction, I felt a sense of pride, a knowledge that my work was reaching people, that my vision was resonating, that my brand was becoming more than a business—it was becoming a reflection of my journey, a testament to the values that had shaped my life. Yet, even in these moments of pride, I remained mindful of the responsibility that came with it, a responsibility to serve my customers with integrity, to uphold the values that had guided me, to build a business that was both successful and righteous.

Each success, each milestone, became a reminder of the blessings that Allah had granted me, a reminder that my journey, though challenging, was guided not by my own strength but by the blessings of Allah, blessings that were both a gift and a responsibility, a chance to serve, to honor the legacy of my family, to build a life that would bring both success and honor.

In moments of doubt, I would turn to prayer, seeking guidance, strength, and understanding, a reminder that my journey was not mine alone but a path that had been set for me, a journey that required both resilience and humility, a journey that would bring both success and honor, a journey that would reflect the goodness of Allah. And as I embraced this strength, I felt a renewed sense of purpose, a commitment to build a life that would bring both success and honor, a life that would reflect the values of Islam and the legacy of my family.

In the quiet moments, I reflected on the meaning of wealth, of the true purpose behind each coin earned, each sale made. Wealth, I had come to understand, was not merely a measure of one's success; it was a tool, a means of supporting others, of bringing good into the world, a chance to uplift those who were less fortunate. In this realization, I felt a sense of humility, a reminder that my journey, though personal, was also a means of service, a way to honor Allah through the blessings I had been granted.

Each coin, each profit, became a symbol of the responsibility I bore, a reminder that wealth, when pursued with humility, becomes more than a measure of success—it becomes a gift, a chance to bring blessings to others, a means of building a legacy that would bring honor to my family and to Allah. And as I embraced this purpose, I felt a sense of peace, a commitment to use my wealth in a way that was both meaningful and righteous, a commitment to support those who needed it, to bring good into the world, to use my success as a means of serving others.

With each step forward, I felt a renewed sense of purpose, a commitment to build a life that would bring both success and honor, a life that would reflect the values of Islam, values of honesty, humility, and compassion. And as I continued on this path, I resolved to trust in Allah, to believe that every challenge, every victory, was a blessing, a chance to grow, to learn, to become the person I was meant to be.

As my business continued to grow, I began to understand the true nature of leadership, a quality that went beyond mere authority, beyond the power to make decisions. Leadership, I realized, was a responsibility, a trust placed upon one to guide, to serve, to uplift others. In the role of a business owner, I found myself faced with choices that affected not only myself but my customers, my suppliers, and those who depended on my products. Each decision became a chance to lead with integrity, to make choices that reflected the values of Islam, the principles of honesty, humility, and compassion.

The path of leadership was filled with challenges, with moments that tested my resolve, that demanded both patience and resilience. There were times when delays in shipments tested the trust of my customers, times when suppliers faltered, times when I had to communicate challenges that were beyond my control. In these moments, I was reminded of the importance of honesty, of the need to communicate openly, to be transparent with those who had placed their trust in me. For true leadership, I learned, is not about hiding one's weaknesses but about acknowledging them, about building trust through honesty and consistency.

Each day, as I navigated these responsibilities, I felt a sense of humility, a reminder that my journey was not for myself alone but for the benefit of those who had placed their faith in my business, those who had chosen to support my vision. In each interaction, I saw an opportunity to serve, to offer a product that was not only valuable but meaningful, a product that would reflect the values that had guided me, values that reminded me that true success is measured not by profit alone but by the impact one has upon the lives of others.

And though the journey was challenging, though the path of leadership required both resilience and humility, I felt a quiet strength, a belief that, with patience and faith, I could build a business that would bring both success and honor, a business that would reflect the goodness of Allah and the values that had shaped my life. For in each decision, in each act of service, I saw a reminder that my journey was guided by a wisdom far greater than my own, a wisdom that would lead me to a life that would bring both profit and purpose.

CHAPTER 5: DISCOVERING NEW PATHS

The journey into coding began as an inkling, a quiet whisper of curiosity that soon transformed into an eager pursuit. As I watched videos, read tutorials, and pored over online resources, I found myself captivated by the world of technology—a world where creativity and logic intertwined, where one could craft entire experiences with mere lines of code. My first project, though humble, felt like a gateway, a chance to harness this skill for something meaningful, something that would align with my vision of a life built upon purpose and principle.

This first project was simple, nothing more than a basic application with limited functionality, yet in its creation, I felt a spark of possibility, a sense that this skill could become more than a pastime. It could become a tool, a means of creating something that could support my vision, a platform that would not only serve my own ambitions but provide a service, a benefit to others. With each step forward, as I crafted my first lines of code, I felt a sense of accomplishment, a knowledge that I was building a foundation, a skill set that would allow me to bring my ideas to life in a way that was both tangible and impactful.

As I delved deeper into this new world, I found myself eager to share my ideas, to seek the insights and support of those who had been with me from the beginning—Aman and Maqsood, my friends and brothers in spirit, who had always believed in me even when I doubted myself. Together, we gathered one evening, our conversations flowing with a blend of excitement and possibility, our minds weaving ideas that spoke of ambition tempered by purpose, of a business that could honor both our dreams and our values.

The three of us sat in our familiar spot beneath the stars, discussing the potential of the app, brainstorming features and possibilities, exploring ways in which we might create something that was both useful and halal. Aman, ever the pragmatist, suggested practical features, ways in which the app could serve a purpose, ways in which it could stand out in a crowded market. Maqsood, with his boundless optimism, encouraged me to dream big, to consider the possibilities, to believe in the potential of my work.

As our conversation unfolded, I felt a renewed sense of purpose, a belief that this journey, though uncertain, was one that I was meant to walk, a journey that would allow me to build a life that was both successful and righteous. And though the path was challenging, I knew that with the support of my friends, with the guidance of Allah, I could find a way forward, a way to build something that would honor both my ambitions and my faith.

With a heart full of excitement, I committed myself to learning, to mastering the skills that would allow me to bring my vision to life. Each day became a blend of study and practice, of trial and error, as I worked tirelessly to understand the intricacies of coding, to learn the languages and techniques that would transform my ideas into reality. I spent hours at my computer, my fingers flying over the keys, my mind focused on the task at hand, determined to overcome each challenge, to master each new concept.

In those quiet hours, I found a joy that went beyond achievement, a satisfaction that came not from the end result but from the process itself, from the act of learning, of growing, of building something from the ground up. And though the journey was challenging, though each step required patience and resilience, I felt a sense of purpose, a belief that this skill, this dedication, would become a tool, a means of achieving my dreams in a way that was both meaningful and honorable.

With each lesson, with each piece of knowledge, I felt a growing confidence, a belief that I was capable, that I could build something of value, something that would bring both profit and purpose. And though the road was long, I resolved to approach each challenge with a heart full of determination, a spirit that trusted in Allah's guidance, a faith that believed in the goodness of this path.

As my skills grew, I began working on my first app project—a simple shopping app, an idea that, though humble, held within it the potential to bring value, to create a source of income that was both halal and sustainable. The concept was straightforward, a platform where users could browse products, compare prices, and make purchases, yet in its simplicity, I saw an opportunity to serve, to create a tool that could offer both convenience and utility.

Each line of code became a step forward, each feature a piece of the vision that was taking shape within me, a vision of a business that would honor both my values and my ambitions. I spent hours crafting the interface, designing features that would make the app intuitive, accessible, a platform that would be both practical and ethical, a space where users could find products that were halal, that reflected the principles of honesty and integrity.

And as I worked, I felt a sense of accomplishment, a knowledge that I was building something of value, something that would bring both success and meaning, a reminder that my journey, though challenging, was one that was blessed, a gift that allowed me to grow, to learn, to become the person I was meant to be. For in each line of code, in each feature, I saw a reflection of the values that had guided me, values that reminded me that true success is measured not by wealth alone but by the impact one has upon the lives of others.

Yet, even as my project took shape, I encountered a challenge that tested my patience and resolve—the struggle to understand the technical knowledge required to bring my vision to life. Coding, though exhilarating, was also a complex art, a skill that required precision, patience, and an unyielding commitment to detail. With each feature I built, each piece of functionality I added, I faced errors, bugs, issues that seemed to defy my understanding, challenges that required both skill and persistence.

The first time my code failed, I felt a wave of frustration, a sense of inadequacy, a fear that perhaps I had overreached, that my vision was beyond my capabilities. Yet, even in this moment of doubt, I felt a quiet reminder, a call to trust in the process, to believe that every challenge was a lesson, a chance to grow, to learn, to build resilience. And as I faced each error, each setback, I reminded myself of the commitment I had made, the promise to build something that was both valuable and halal, a platform that would serve a purpose, that would bring blessings upon those who used it.

With each attempt, each failure, I grew more determined, more committed to overcoming these challenges, to building something that would honor both my dreams and my values. For in each line of code, in each feature, I saw a reflection of the journey that had brought me to this point, a journey that had been filled with lessons, with moments of growth, with reminders that true success is measured not by wealth alone but by the impact one has upon the lives of others.

In the midst of these challenges, I found strength in the support of my friends, in the encouragement of Aman and Maqsood, whose belief in me never wavered, whose presence reminded me that I was not alone, that my journey was one that we walked together, a journey that was filled with both struggle and joy, with moments of frustration and moments of triumph. They listened patiently as I spoke of the errors I faced, of the challenges that seemed insurmountable, offering words of encouragement, reminders of the progress I had made, of the vision that had inspired me from the beginning.

With their support, I found a renewed sense of purpose, a belief that my journey, though challenging, was one that I was meant to walk, a journey that would allow me to build a life that was both successful and righteous. And though the path was uncertain, I knew that with the support of my friends, with the guidance of Allah, I could find a way forward, a way to build something that would honor both my ambitions and my faith.

In their presence, I felt a quiet strength, a resilience that carried me through the moments of doubt, a reminder that my journey, though filled with challenges, was a gift, an opportunity to grow, to learn, to become the person I was meant to be. For in each struggle, in each moment of frustration, I saw a chance to refine my vision, to build a business that would bring both profit and purpose, a business that would honor both my family and my faith.

As my app began to take shape, I found myself reflecting upon the purpose that had driven me to start this journey—a purpose that was as much about serving others as it was about building a successful business. In a world driven by competition, by the pursuit of profit, I had come to see that my vision was different, that my aim was not merely to achieve wealth but to create something of value, something that would bring blessings not only upon myself but upon those who used my app. This purpose became my guiding light, a reminder that every decision, every feature, every choice I made was a chance to reflect the values of honesty, integrity, and compassion.

Each day, as I coded, as I crafted the features that would make my app unique, I kept this purpose in mind, striving to create a platform that would serve others, that would offer convenience, value, and utility. I envisioned a space where users could shop with confidence, where they could find products that were halal, that met the standards of ethical sourcing and fair trade, a space that would honor the values of Islam in both principle and practice. And as this vision took shape, I felt a sense of pride, a knowledge that my work was a reflection of my journey, a testament to the lessons I had learned, the values that had been instilled within me.

In moments of doubt, when the challenges seemed overwhelming, I would remind myself of this purpose, of the commitment I had made to build something that was both meaningful and honorable, a business that would serve others, that would reflect the goodness of Allah. And though the path was challenging, though each step required patience and perseverance, I felt a quiet strength, a belief that with faith and effort, I could bring this vision to life, a vision that would bring both success and honor, a vision that would bring blessings upon all those who used it.

As my app grew, so too did my understanding of resilience, a quality that had become both a necessity and a virtue, a reminder that true success is often measured not by the absence of failure but by the willingness to continue in the face of obstacles. Coding, though rewarding, was a discipline that required patience, a commitment to overcoming each error, each bug, each unexpected challenge that arose. In this journey, I found myself growing not only in skill but in character, learning to embrace the process, to trust that every setback was a lesson, every challenge a chance to grow stronger.

The errors I encountered were not merely technical issues; they were opportunities, chances to refine my work, to improve my understanding, to deepen my commitment to the vision I held. With each bug fixed, each problem solved, I felt a sense of accomplishment, a reminder that my journey, though challenging, was one that was blessed, a path that was leading me toward a life that would bring both success and meaning, a life that would honor both my ambitions and my values.

In moments of frustration, I would remind myself of the purpose that had driven me from the beginning, a purpose that was as much about serving others as it was about achieving success. For in each line of code, in each feature, I saw a reflection of the journey that had brought me to this point, a journey that had been filled with lessons, with moments of growth, with reminders that true success is measured not by wealth alone but by the impact one has upon the lives of others.

As the app neared completion, I found myself filled with a mixture of excitement and trepidation, a blend of anticipation and uncertainty that left me both eager and cautious. I had poured my heart into this project, had invested countless hours, had faced and overcome countless challenges, yet as the launch date approached, I felt a quiet fear, a reminder of the uncertainty that lay ahead. Would users embrace my app? Would they find it valuable, meaningful, a platform that served their needs? These questions lingered in my mind, casting shadows over the excitement that had carried me through each step of this journey.

In these moments of doubt, I turned once more to prayer, seeking guidance, strength, and reassurance, a reminder that my journey was not mine alone, that it was guided by a wisdom far greater than my own. I prayed for success, for blessings upon my work, for the strength to face whatever challenges lay ahead, for the resilience to continue, to trust in Allah's plan, to believe that every effort, every sacrifice, would bear fruit in its own time. And as I prayed, I felt a sense of peace, a quiet confidence that my journey, though uncertain, was blessed, a path that would bring both success and honor, a path that would bring blessings upon all those who used my app.

With each prayer, I felt my fears recede, replaced by a quiet determination, a belief that my journey was one that I was meant to walk, a journey that would allow me to build a life that was both successful and righteous. And though the road was challenging, I knew that with the support of my friends, with the guidance of Allah, I could find a way forward, a way to build something that would honor both my ambitions and my faith.

The day of the app's launch arrived with a blend of excitement and nervous energy, a sense of anticipation that left me both eager and apprehensive. I had worked tirelessly to bring this vision to life, had crafted each feature with care, had tested and retested every function, yet as the app went live, as the first users began to engage, I found myself filled with questions, with doubts, with hopes that my work would resonate, that it would bring value, that it would serve the purpose I had envisioned.

As the first reviews came in, I felt a wave of relief, a sense of accomplishment, a knowledge that my efforts had borne fruit, that my app was making a difference, that it was bringing value to those who used it. The feedback was encouraging, filled with words of appreciation, with comments that spoke of convenience, of ease, of a platform that met their needs, that offered a service that was both useful and ethical. In each review, I saw a reflection of my journey, a testament to the work I had poured into this project, a reminder that my journey, though filled with challenges, was one that was blessed, a gift that allowed me to serve, to contribute, to build something meaningful.

Yet, even as I celebrated these successes, I remained mindful of the responsibility that came with it, a responsibility to serve my users with integrity, to uphold the values that had guided me, to build a platform that would continue to bring blessings upon all those who used it. For true success, I realized, was not measured by the launch of an app but by the impact it had upon the lives of others, by the goodness it brought into the world, by the blessings it bestowed upon those who trusted in my work.

With each new user, each new interaction, I felt a renewed sense of purpose, a commitment to continue, to refine, to improve, to ensure that my app would remain a platform that honored both my ambitions and my faith. And as I embraced this responsibility, I felt a quiet confidence, a belief that my journey, though challenging, was one that I was meant to walk, a journey that would bring both success and honor, a journey that would reflect the goodness of Allah and the values that had shaped my life.

In the weeks that followed the launch, I experienced the ebb and flow of success, the ups and downs that define the journey of entrepreneurship, the moments of triumph and the challenges that tested my resolve. There were days when the app performed beyond my expectations, when the user count grew steadily, when each review was a testament to the value it brought, a reflection of the purpose that had guided me. And then, there were days when issues arose, when users reported bugs, when the app experienced technical difficulties that required both patience and diligence to resolve.

In these moments, I found myself reminded of the importance of humility, of the need to approach each challenge with a heart that was both open and resilient, a heart that trusted in the process, that believed in the goodness of the journey. Each issue became an opportunity, a chance to refine my work, to improve my understanding, to deepen my commitment to the vision I held. And as I embraced these challenges, I felt a sense of growth, a knowledge that my journey, though filled with obstacles, was leading me toward a life that was both meaningful and honorable, a life that would bring both success and blessings upon all those who used my app.

With each step forward, I felt a renewed sense of purpose, a commitment to build a platform that would bring both profit and purpose, a platform that would reflect the values of Islam and the legacy of my family. And though the road was long, I resolved to approach each challenge with humility, to trust in Allah's guidance, to believe that every effort, every sacrifice, would bear fruit in its own time.

As my app found its footing among users, I came to understand the importance of adaptability—the need to adjust, to evolve, to respond to feedback in a way that honored both my vision and my users' experiences. The process of refining the app, of addressing user concerns, became a journey in itself, a path that required both patience and humility, a willingness to admit shortcomings, to learn, to grow in ways that went beyond coding and technical skill.

Each piece of feedback was a lesson, a reminder that my work, though personal, was also a service, a gift that I had been entrusted with, a platform that others depended upon. I found myself reviewing each comment, each suggestion, with a heart that was both open and discerning, a heart that sought to improve, to refine, to create a platform that was truly valuable. And though this process required both time and effort, I felt a sense of peace, a knowledge that my work was meaningful, that it was bringing blessings upon those who used it.

In moments of frustration, when the challenges seemed overwhelming, I reminded myself of the values that had guided me, values of honesty, of humility, of a commitment to building something that would honor both my faith and my users. For in each adjustment, in each improvement, I saw a reflection of the journey that had brought me to this point, a journey that had been filled with lessons, with moments of growth, with reminders that true success is measured not by wealth alone but by the impact one has upon the lives of others.

And though the road was challenging, though each step required patience and perseverance, I felt a quiet strength, a belief that with faith and effort, I could build a platform that would bring both success and honor, a platform that would reflect the values of Islam and the goodness of Allah.

With each improvement, I felt my confidence grow, a quiet assurance that I was building something of value, something that would bring blessings upon all those who used it. The journey, though challenging, was one that had taught me resilience, a quality that had become both a necessity and a virtue, a reminder that true success is often measured not by the absence of failure but by the willingness to continue in the face of obstacles. Coding, though rewarding, was a discipline that required patience, a commitment to overcoming each error, each bug, each unexpected challenge that arose.

In these moments, I found myself reflecting on the concept of intention, a principle that is deeply rooted in Islam, a reminder that one's actions are measured by the heart with which they are undertaken, by the purpose that drives each step. My intention, I realized, was not merely to build a profitable business but to create something that was valuable, meaningful, a platform that would bring blessings upon those who used it, a reminder that my work, though personal, was also a service, a gift that I had been entrusted with.

And as I embraced this intention, I felt a sense of peace, a quiet confidence that my journey, though uncertain, was guided by a wisdom far greater than my own, a wisdom that would lead me to a life that was both successful and honorable, a life that would reflect the values of Islam and the goodness of Allah. For in each effort, in each moment of struggle, I saw a chance to build something that would bring both profit and purpose, a platform that would honor both my ambitions and my faith.

In the months following the app's launch, I encountered the ebb and flow of success, the ups and downs that define the journey of entrepreneurship, the moments of triumph and the challenges that tested my resolve. There were days when the app performed beyond my expectations, when the user count grew steadily, when each review was a testament to the value it brought, a reflection of the purpose that had guided me. And then, there were days when issues arose, when users reported bugs, when the app experienced technical difficulties that required both patience and diligence to resolve.

In these moments, I found myself reminded of the importance of humility, of the need to approach each challenge with a heart that was both open and resilient, a heart that trusted in the process, that believed in the goodness of the journey. Each issue became an opportunity, a chance to refine my work, to improve my understanding, to deepen my commitment to the vision I held. And as I embraced these challenges, I felt a sense of growth, a knowledge that my journey, though filled with obstacles, was leading me toward a life that was both meaningful and honorable, a life that would bring both success and blessings upon all those who used my app.

With each step forward, I felt a renewed sense of purpose, a commitment to build a platform that would bring both profit and purpose, a platform that would reflect the values of Islam and the legacy of my family. And though the road was long, I resolved to approach each challenge with humility, to trust in Allah's guidance, to believe that every effort, every sacrifice, would bear fruit in its own time.

As the app continued to gain traction, I began to understand the impact of my work, the way in which my vision was resonating with users, the way in which each feature, each function, was serving a purpose, a need that had been waiting to be met. In moments of reflection, I found myself filled with gratitude, a knowledge that my journey, though challenging, was one that was blessed, a gift that allowed me to serve, to contribute, to build something meaningful.

Each review, each comment, was a reminder of the blessings that Allah had granted me, a reminder that my journey, though uncertain, was guided not by my own strength but by the goodness of Allah, by a wisdom that was leading me to a life that would bring both success and honor, a life that would bring blessings upon all those who used my app. For true success, I realized, was not measured by the number of downloads or the profits earned, but by the value it brought into the lives of others, by the goodness it brought into the world, by the blessings it bestowed upon those who trusted in my work.

In these moments of gratitude, I found myself returning once more to the teachings of Islam, to the principles of honesty, humility, and compassion, values that reminded me that true success is measured not by wealth alone but by the impact one has upon the lives of others. And as I embraced these teachings, I felt a renewed sense of purpose, a commitment to build a platform that was not merely profitable but meaningful, a platform that would reflect the values of Islam and the legacy of my family.

In the midst of these successes, I encountered a challenge that tested my commitment, a reminder that every journey is filled with moments that demand resilience, moments that require both strength and faith. It began as a small issue—a glitch in the app that affected only a handful of users, an error that seemed minor yet had the potential to grow, to disrupt the experience of those who depended upon my work. At first, I felt a wave of frustration, a sense of inadequacy, a fear that perhaps I had overlooked something, that my work was not as polished as I had believed.

But as I confronted this challenge, as I sought to resolve the issue, I found myself reminded of the importance of patience, of the need to approach each problem with a heart that was both humble and resilient, a heart that trusted in the process, that believed in the goodness of the journey. For each issue, each challenge, was an opportunity, a chance to refine my work, to improve my understanding, to deepen my commitment to the vision I held.

And as I worked to resolve the glitch, I felt a sense of growth, a knowledge that my journey, though filled with obstacles, was leading me toward a life that was both meaningful and honorable, a life that would bring both success and blessings upon all those who used my app. For in each challenge, in each moment of struggle, I saw a reflection of the values that had guided me, values that reminded me that true success is measured not by wealth alone but by the impact one has upon the lives of others.

With each step forward, I felt a renewed sense of purpose, a commitment to build a platform that would bring both profit and purpose, a platform that would reflect the values of Islam and the legacy of my family.

As my app continued to grow, I began to understand the profound role that community played in shaping my journey. The feedback I received from users became more than just comments; it became a guiding light, a source of insight that allowed me to see my work through the eyes of those it served. Each suggestion, each request, each critique was a reflection of the needs, the hopes, the desires of those who had placed their trust in my vision. And as I read through each piece of feedback, I felt a sense of responsibility, a commitment to ensure that my work would continue to bring value, to meet the expectations of those who believed in its purpose.

The journey of refining my app became a journey of service, a path that required both patience and humility, a willingness to listen, to learn, to adapt. I found myself reaching out to users, engaging in conversations, seeking to understand their experiences, their needs, their dreams. In these conversations, I felt a sense of connection, a reminder that my work was not mine alone but a shared vision, a platform that existed not merely to profit but to provide, to uplift, to offer a service that was both valuable and meaningful.

With each update, with each improvement, I felt a sense of purpose, a belief that my journey, though challenging, was one that was blessed, a path that allowed me to grow, to serve, to build something that would bring both success and honor, something that would reflect the values of Islam, values of honesty, humility, and compassion. And though the road was filled with challenges, I resolved to approach each step with humility, to trust in Allah's guidance, to believe that every effort, every sacrifice, would bear fruit in its own time, that my work would continue to bring blessings upon all those who used it.

With each update, each improvement, I felt a renewed sense of commitment, a dedication to building a platform that would not only serve my users but would stand as a reflection of my faith, my values, my purpose. In the world of business, it is often easy to lose oneself, to become consumed by profit, by the pursuit of growth, by the desire to achieve. Yet, as I navigated this journey, I found myself grounded by the teachings of Islam, by the principles of integrity, of humility, of service. Each decision, each choice, became a test, a chance to prove my commitment to the values that had shaped my life.

I realized that success, in its truest form, was not measured by the wealth one accumulated but by the goodness one brought into the world, by the blessings one bestowed upon others, by the impact one had upon the lives of those around them. My app, I understood, was not merely a tool for profit but a platform that had the power to serve, to uplift, to bring value into the lives of its users. And as I embraced this understanding, I felt a renewed sense of purpose, a commitment to continue, to refine, to ensure that my work would remain a source of blessings, a platform that would honor both my ambitions and my faith.

In moments of doubt, when the challenges seemed insurmountable, I would remind myself of the purpose that had guided me from the beginning, a purpose that was as much about serving others as it was about achieving success. For in each line of code, in each feature, I saw a reflection of the journey that had brought me to this point, a journey that had been filled with lessons, with moments of growth, with reminders that true success is measured not by wealth alone but by the impact one has upon the lives of others.

As the app evolved, so too did my understanding of resilience, a quality that had become both a necessity and a virtue, a reminder that true success is often measured not by the absence of failure but by the willingness to continue in the face of obstacles. Coding, though rewarding, was a discipline that required patience, a commitment to overcoming each error, each bug, each unexpected challenge that arose. In this journey, I found myself growing not only in skill but in character, learning to embrace the process, to trust that every setback was a lesson, every challenge a chance to grow stronger.

The errors I encountered were not merely technical issues; they were opportunities, chances to refine my work, to improve my understanding, to deepen my commitment to the vision I held. With each bug fixed, each problem solved, I felt a sense of accomplishment, a reminder that my journey, though challenging, was one that was blessed, a path that was leading me toward a life that would bring both success and meaning, a life that would honor both my ambitions and my values.

In moments of frustration, I would remind myself of the purpose that had driven me from the beginning, a purpose that was as much about serving others as it was about achieving success. For in each line of code, in each feature, I saw a reflection of the journey that had brought me to this point, a journey that had been filled with lessons, with moments of growth, with reminders that true success is measured not by wealth alone but by the impact one has upon the lives of others.

As the app neared completion, I found myself filled with a mixture of excitement and trepidation, a blend of anticipation and uncertainty that left me both eager and cautious. I had poured my heart into this project, had invested countless hours, had faced and overcome countless challenges, yet as the launch date approached, I felt a quiet fear, a reminder of the uncertainty that lay ahead. Would users embrace my app? Would they find it valuable, meaningful, a platform that served their needs? These questions lingered in my mind, casting shadows over the excitement that had carried me through each step of this journey.

In these moments of doubt, I turned once more to prayer, seeking guidance, strength, and reassurance, a reminder that my journey was not mine alone, that it was guided by a wisdom far greater than my own. I prayed for success, for blessings upon my work, for the strength to face whatever challenges lay ahead, for the resilience to continue, to trust in Allah's plan, to believe that every effort, every sacrifice, would bear fruit in its own time. And as I prayed, I felt a sense of peace, a quiet confidence that my journey, though uncertain, was blessed, a path that would bring both success and honor, a path that would bring blessings upon all those who used my app.

With each prayer, I felt my fears recede, replaced by a quiet determination, a belief that my journey was one that I was meant to walk, a journey that would allow me to build a life that was both successful and righteous. And though the road was challenging, I knew that with the support of my friends, with the guidance of Allah, I could find a way forward, a way to build something that would honor both my ambitions and my faith.

The day of the app's launch arrived with a blend of excitement and nervous energy, a sense of anticipation that left me both eager and apprehensive. I had worked tirelessly to bring this vision to life, had crafted each feature with care, had tested and retested every function, yet as the app went live, as the first users began to engage, I found myself filled with questions, with doubts, with hopes that my work would resonate, that it would bring value, that it would serve the purpose I had envisioned.

As the first reviews came in, I felt a wave of relief, a sense of accomplishment, a knowledge that my efforts had borne fruit, that my app was making a difference, that it was bringing value to those who used it. The feedback was encouraging, filled with words of appreciation, with comments that spoke of convenience, of ease, of a platform that met their needs, that offered a service that was both useful and ethical. In each review, I saw a reflection of my journey, a testament to the work I had poured into this project, a reminder that my journey, though filled with challenges, was one that was blessed, a gift that allowed me to serve, to contribute, to build something meaningful.

Yet, even as I celebrated these successes, I remained mindful of the responsibility that came with it, a responsibility to serve my users with integrity, to uphold the values that had guided me, to build a platform that would continue to bring blessings upon all those who used it. For true success, I realized, was not measured by the launch of an app but by the impact it had upon the lives of others, by the goodness it brought into the world, by the blessings it bestowed upon those who trusted in my work.

CHAPTER 6: THE FRUITS OF FAITH AND RESILIENCE

The early days after the app's launch felt like the gentle unfolding of a new dawn, each day bringing with it the steady, rewarding rhythm of purpose fulfilled. With every new user, every piece of feedback, I felt my work take on a life of its own, as though the seeds of patience and effort I had sown were beginning to bear fruit. It was a quiet, almost reverent joy, not the sudden thrill of riches or renown, but the calm satisfaction of knowing that each step forward was a testament to resilience, a tribute to the values that had shaped my path.

My heart felt full, not only with the success that was beginning to blossom but with gratitude—gratitude for the trials that had tested me, for the moments of doubt that had taught me strength, for the guidance of Allah that had never faltered. In those early days, I would often find myself pausing, reflecting on the journey that had brought me to this point, a journey that had been as much about faith as it was about ambition. For while the rewards of my work were sweet, I understood that true success was not a treasure measured in coins but in contentment, in the peace of knowing one's path aligns with one's purpose.

With each quiet moment of gratitude, I felt a renewed sense of purpose, a commitment to nurture this work, to honor the principles of honesty, integrity, and compassion that had guided me from the beginning. And though the road ahead was still long, I knew that each step would bring me closer to a life that was both successful and righteous, a life that would reflect the goodness of Allah and the values that had shaped me.

As the days turned into weeks, I began to see the impact of my work, the way in which my app was resonating with users, the way in which it was meeting their needs, fulfilling a purpose that was both practical and profound. Each review, each message, was a reminder of the blessings that Allah had granted me, a reminder that my journey, though challenging, was one that was blessed, a gift that allowed me to serve, to contribute, to build something meaningful.

In these moments of reflection, I felt a sense of humility, a reminder that true success is not merely a personal achievement but a responsibility, a trust that Allah has placed in our hands, a chance to use our talents, our efforts, to bring good into the world. My app, I understood, was not merely a tool for profit but a platform that had the power to serve, to uplift, to bring value into the lives of its users. And as I embraced this understanding, I felt a renewed sense of purpose, a commitment to continue, to refine, to ensure that my work would remain a source of blessings, a platform that would honor both my ambitions and my faith.

With each new user, each new interaction, I felt a sense of connection, a belief that my journey, though filled with challenges, was one that was meant to bring both profit and purpose, a reminder that true wealth is measured not by the coins in one's hand but by the goodness in one's heart, by the impact one has upon the lives of others.

As the app grew, I found myself faced with new challenges, responsibilities that went beyond the technical realm, questions of ethics, of integrity, of ensuring that my work would continue to honor the values that had guided me from the beginning. Success, I realized, was not a single moment of achievement but a series of choices, each one a test of my character, a chance to prove my commitment to the principles of honesty, humility, and service that had been instilled within me since childhood.

In these moments of decision, I found myself turning once more to the teachings of Islam, to the principles of justice, of compassion, of a commitment to serve. I understood that each choice, each action, was an opportunity to reflect these values, to build a platform that was not only profitable but ethical, a platform that would bring blessings upon all those who used it, a platform that would honor the legacy of my family and the values of my faith.

With each decision, I felt a renewed sense of responsibility, a reminder that my journey, though personal, was also a means of service, a chance to honor Allah through the blessings I had been granted. And though the road was challenging, I felt a quiet strength, a belief that with patience and humility, I could build something that would bring both success and honor, something that would reflect the values of Islam, values of honesty, humility, and compassion.

The path of success was, I soon discovered, not without its temptations. In the world of business, the allure of profit, the pursuit of growth, the desire to achieve can often overshadow the values that one holds dear, can lead one astray from the principles that had once guided each step. Yet, as I navigated this journey, I found myself grounded by the teachings of Islam, by the reminder that true success is measured not by wealth alone but by the goodness one brings into the world, by the blessings one bestows upon others.

Each day became a test, a chance to prove my commitment to the values that had shaped my life, a reminder that my journey was not for myself alone but for the benefit of those who had placed their trust in my work, those who depended upon my platform, those who believed in the vision I held. In each choice, in each action, I saw an opportunity to build a business that was both profitable and meaningful, a business that would reflect the values of Islam, values of honesty, humility, and service.

And though the temptations were many, though the road was filled with moments that tested my resolve, I felt a quiet strength, a knowledge that my journey, though challenging, was one that was blessed, a gift that allowed me to grow, to learn, to build something that would bring both success and blessings upon all those who used it.

With each step forward, I began to understand the deeper purpose of my journey, a purpose that was as much about serving others as it was about achieving personal success. My app, I realized, was not merely a product but a platform that could bring value, a tool that could offer convenience, ease, a means of fulfilling needs in a way that was both ethical and meaningful. This understanding filled me with a sense of responsibility, a commitment to ensure that my work would continue to reflect the values of Islam, values that reminded me that true success is measured not by wealth alone but by the impact one has upon the lives of others.

With this understanding came a renewed sense of purpose, a belief that my journey, though challenging, was one that was meant to bring both profit and blessings, a reminder that true wealth is not a treasure measured in coins but in the goodness one brings into the world, the blessings one bestows upon others. Each day, as I worked, as I crafted each feature, each function, I felt a quiet strength, a knowledge that my journey was guided not by my own strength but by the blessings of Allah, by a wisdom that was leading me to a life that would bring both success and honor, a life that would reflect the values of Islam and the legacy of my family.

With each moment of reflection, I felt a sense of peace, a reminder that my journey, though personal, was also a means of service, a path that would allow me to bring both profit and purpose, a path that would honor both my ambitions and my faith.

As the weeks turned into months, I felt the weight of my responsibilities grow, a reminder that each step forward was a chance to serve, to contribute, to build something meaningful. Success, I understood, was not merely a personal achievement but a trust, a responsibility to uphold the values that had guided me, to build a business that would bring blessings upon those who used it, to ensure that my platform would remain a source of value, a source of good, a reflection of the principles of honesty, integrity, and compassion.

In these moments of reflection, I found myself returning to the teachings of Islam, to the reminder that wealth, when pursued without humility, becomes hollow, a shadow of true success. I understood that my journey, though filled with challenges, was a gift, a path that allowed me to grow, to learn, to build something that would bring both success and blessings upon all those who used it. And as I embraced this understanding, I felt a renewed sense of purpose, a commitment to build a platform that was both profitable and meaningful, a platform that would honor both my ambitions and my faith.

In moments of doubt, when the challenges seemed insurmountable, I would remind myself of the purpose that had guided me from the beginning, a purpose that was as much about serving others as it was about achieving success. For in each line of code, in each feature, I saw a reflection of the journey that had brought me to this point, a journey that had been filled with lessons, with moments of growth, with reminders that true success is measured not by wealth alone but by the impact one has upon the lives of others.

In those quiet hours when the world seemed still, I often found myself contemplating the nature of wealth, of what it truly meant to be successful. Success, as I had come to understand, was not merely the accumulation of riches but a trust, a responsibility to use one's blessings in a way that brought goodness, that honored the values of honesty, humility, and compassion. Each day, as my app continued to grow, as my user base expanded, I felt the weight of this responsibility, a reminder that my journey was not for myself alone but a path that allowed me to serve, to uplift, to contribute to something greater.

The wealth that my work had begun to yield was a gift, a blessing that held within it the potential to bring joy, to fulfill dreams, to support those who were less fortunate. And as I embraced this understanding, I felt a sense of gratitude, a knowledge that my journey, though filled with challenges, was one that was blessed, a gift that allowed me to use my talents, my efforts, in a way that would bring both success and blessings upon all those who used it.

In these moments of reflection, I felt a renewed sense of purpose, a commitment to use my wealth in a way that would honor both my family and my faith, a way that would reflect the values of Islam, values that reminded me that true success is measured not by wealth alone but by the impact one has upon the lives of others. And though the path was challenging, though each step required patience and humility, I felt a quiet strength, a belief that with faith and resilience, I could continue to build a platform that would bring both profit and purpose, a platform that would honor both my ambitions and my values.

The joy of success, as I discovered, was best shared, best savored in the presence of those who had walked this journey with me, who had believed in me even when I doubted myself. My friends Aman and Maqsood had been my constant companions, my brothers in spirit, whose support had been a source of strength, a reminder that my journey, though personal, was not mine alone but a shared vision, a reflection of the values we held dear. Together, we had dreamt, we had planned, we had worked to bring this app to life, and now, as it began to bear fruit, I felt a deep sense of gratitude, a desire to share these blessings with those who had been by my side.

One evening, as we gathered to reflect on the journey we had walked together, I found myself thanking them, expressing the gratitude that had filled my heart, a gratitude that was as much for their support as it was for their belief, their encouragement, their unwavering faith in my vision. Their words, though humble, were a reminder of the importance of friendship, of the bonds that had carried us through moments of struggle, of doubt, of uncertainty.

In their presence, I felt a quiet peace, a reminder that success, in its truest form, is a shared joy, a blessing that grows when it is given, a gift that brings not only wealth but meaning, fulfillment, a sense of purpose that goes beyond profit, beyond achievement. And as I looked upon my friends, I felt a renewed commitment, a belief that my journey, though challenging, was one that was blessed, a path that would allow me to continue to grow, to serve, to build a life that would bring both success and blessings upon all those who walked it with me.

As my business continued to grow, so too did the sense of responsibility that came with it, a reminder that every blessing, every success, was both a gift and a trust, a chance to bring goodness into the world, to serve, to uplift, to contribute to a legacy that would honor both my family and my faith. I found myself thinking about the impact of my work, the way in which each feature, each function, was an opportunity to reflect the values that had guided me, values that reminded me that true wealth is measured not by the coins in one's hand but by the goodness in one's heart, by the blessings one brings into the lives of others.

In moments of reflection, I felt a renewed sense of purpose, a commitment to continue, to refine, to ensure that my app would remain a source of value, a platform that would bring both convenience and blessings upon all those who used it. And though the path was filled with challenges, I felt a quiet strength, a belief that with patience and humility, I could build a business that was both profitable and meaningful, a business that would reflect the goodness of Allah and the values that had shaped my life.

In these quiet moments, I would often find myself praying, asking for guidance, for strength, for the wisdom to make choices that would honor both my ambitions and my faith, choices that would reflect the values of Islam, values of honesty, humility, and compassion. And as I prayed, I felt a peace, a quiet confidence that my journey, though uncertain, was guided by a wisdom far greater than my own, a wisdom that would lead me to a life that would bring both success and honor, a life that would reflect the legacy of my family and the teachings of my faith.

With each step forward, I came to understand the true meaning of success, a meaning that was as much about serving others as it was about achieving personal fulfillment. My app, I realized, was more than a product—it was a tool that could bring value, a platform that could offer convenience, ease, a means of fulfilling needs in a way that was both ethical and meaningful. This understanding filled me with a sense of responsibility, a commitment to ensure that my work would continue to reflect the values of Islam, values that reminded me that true success is measured not by wealth alone but by the impact one has upon the lives of others.

In moments of doubt, when the challenges seemed overwhelming, I would remind myself of the purpose that had guided me from the beginning, a purpose that was as much about serving others as it was about achieving success. For in each line of code, in each feature, I saw a reflection of the journey that had brought me to this point, a journey that had been filled with lessons, with moments of growth, with reminders that true success is not a treasure measured in coins but a legacy of kindness, of compassion, of service.

And as I embraced this purpose, I felt a renewed sense of dedication, a belief that my journey, though challenging, was one that was blessed, a path that allowed me to grow, to learn, to build something that would bring both profit and blessings, a reminder that true wealth is measured not by the riches one accumulates but by the blessings one bestows upon others.

The days that followed were filled with a sense of joy, a quiet contentment that came not from the wealth my work had begun to yield but from the knowledge that my journey was one that honored both my ambitions and my faith. Each day became an opportunity, a chance to serve, to uplift, to use my blessings in a way that would bring goodness into the world, that would reflect the values of Islam, values of honesty, humility, and compassion. And as I embraced this purpose, I felt a peace, a quiet strength, a belief that my journey, though challenging, was guided by a wisdom far greater than my own, a wisdom that would lead me to a life that would bring both success and honor, a life that would reflect the teachings of my faith and the legacy of my family.

In these quiet moments, I felt a renewed sense of purpose, a commitment to continue, to refine, to ensure that my app would remain a source of value, a platform that would bring both convenience and blessings upon all those who used it. And though the path was filled with challenges, I felt a quiet strength, a belief that with patience and humility, I could build a business that was both profitable and meaningful, a business that would reflect the goodness of Allah and the values that had shaped my life.

With each prayer, with each moment of gratitude, I felt a renewed commitment to use my blessings in a way that would honor both my family and my faith, a way that would bring blessings upon all those who walked this journey with me, a journey that was as much about serving others as it was about achieving personal success.

As my business continued to expand, I began to see that the true journey of success was not only marked by achievements but by the character one cultivated along the way. In the world of entrepreneurship, it was easy to be swept away by ambition, to be consumed by the desire for more, by the pursuit of wealth and recognition. Yet, as I walked this path, I found myself anchored by the principles that had guided me from the beginning—principles of honesty, humility, and service that reminded me that true success is not a measure of wealth but a reflection of the heart, a testament to one's integrity.

The growth of my platform brought with it new responsibilities, new challenges that tested my commitment to these values. Each day was a reminder that success, when pursued with humility, becomes more than a personal victory—it becomes a blessing that extends beyond oneself, a gift that brings goodness into the lives of others. I felt a renewed sense of purpose, a dedication to continue, to refine, to ensure that my work would remain a source of value, a platform that would honor both my ambitions and my faith, a platform that would bring blessings upon all those who used it.

In these moments of reflection, I felt a deep gratitude for the journey I had walked, a journey that had been filled with lessons, with moments of growth, with challenges that had shaped me, strengthened me, refined my character. For in each challenge, I saw an opportunity, a chance to build a business that was both profitable and meaningful, a business that would reflect the values of Islam, values of honesty, humility, and compassion.

With each passing day, as my app reached new users, as its influence began to grow, I felt the weight of my responsibilities deepen. Success, I realized, was not merely a personal achievement but a trust, a blessing that Allah had placed in my hands, a gift that held within it the power to uplift, to serve, to bring value into the lives of others. This understanding filled me with a sense of humility, a reminder that my journey was not for myself alone but a path that allowed me to contribute to something greater, to honor both my ambitions and my faith.

As I looked upon the platform I had built, I found myself contemplating the potential for expansion, the ways in which I might extend its reach, increase its impact, fulfill the purpose that had guided me from the beginning. Yet, even as I envisioned this growth, I felt a quiet caution, a reminder that true success requires balance, a commitment to stay grounded, to ensure that each step forward remains aligned with the principles of honesty, integrity, and compassion that had shaped my journey.

In moments of doubt, when the challenges seemed insurmountable, I turned to prayer, seeking guidance, strength, and understanding, a reminder that my journey was guided not by my own strength but by the blessings of Allah, by a wisdom that was leading me to a life that would bring both success and honor, a life that would reflect the values of Islam and the legacy of my family. And as I prayed, I felt a renewed commitment, a belief that my journey, though challenging, was one that was blessed, a path that would allow me to grow, to serve, to build something meaningful.

The road to success, as I discovered, was filled not only with achievements but with moments that required introspection, moments that demanded one to pause, to reflect, to ensure that every decision, every step forward, was aligned with the purpose that had driven me from the beginning. As my platform continued to grow, I began to understand the importance of intentionality, the need to approach each choice with a heart that was both discerning and humble, a heart that sought to honor both the trust of my users and the values that had guided me.

Each decision became an opportunity to reflect the values of Islam, to build a business that was not only profitable but ethical, a business that would bring blessings upon all those who used it. I understood that each feature, each function, was a chance to serve, to offer a product that was not only valuable but meaningful, a product that would reflect the principles of honesty, integrity, and compassion that had shaped my life.

In these moments of reflection, I felt a deep sense of gratitude, a knowledge that my journey, though filled with challenges, was one that was blessed, a gift that allowed me to use my talents, my efforts, in a way that would bring both success and blessings, a platform that would honor both my family and my faith. For in each choice, in each action, I saw a reminder that my journey was not mine alone but a shared vision, a reflection of the values that had shaped my life, values of honesty, humility, and service.

In the quiet solitude of the evening, I would often find myself contemplating the nature of wealth, of what it meant to truly be rich. Wealth, as I had come to understand, was not merely a measure of one's possessions but a reflection of one's ability to give, to serve, to uplift others. The wealth that my work had begun to yield was a gift, a blessing that held within it the potential to bring joy, to support, to contribute to the well-being of others. And as I embraced this understanding, I felt a renewed sense of purpose, a commitment to use my blessings in a way that would bring goodness into the world, a way that would reflect the values of Islam, values that reminded me that true success is measured not by wealth alone but by the impact one has upon the lives of others.

With each passing day, I felt a deeper responsibility, a knowledge that my journey, though personal, was also a means of service, a path that allowed me to contribute to something greater, to build a legacy that would bring both success and blessings upon all those who walked it with me. And though the path was filled with challenges, though each step required patience and humility, I felt a quiet strength, a belief that with faith and resilience, I could continue to build a business that would bring both profit and purpose, a business that would honor both my ambitions and my values.

In moments of doubt, I would turn to prayer, seeking guidance, strength, and understanding, a reminder that my journey was guided by a wisdom far greater than my own, a wisdom that was leading me to a life that would bring both success and honor, a life that would reflect the teachings of Islam and the legacy of my family.

As my business continued to grow, so too did the opportunities to give back, to support those who were less fortunate, to use my blessings in a way that would bring goodness into the lives of others. I felt a deep sense of gratitude, a knowledge that my journey, though filled with challenges, was one that was blessed, a gift that allowed me to serve, to contribute, to build something meaningful. Each day became an opportunity, a chance to honor both my family and my faith, to use my talents, my efforts, in a way that would bring both success and blessings, a platform that would bring value into the lives of others.

The wealth that my work had begun to yield was not merely a treasure to be kept but a gift to be shared, a blessing that could bring joy, that could fulfill dreams, that could support those who were less fortunate. And as I embraced this understanding, I felt a renewed sense of purpose, a commitment to use my blessings in a way that would honor both my ambitions and my faith, a way that would bring blessings upon all those who walked this journey with me, a journey that was as much about serving others as it was about achieving personal success.

With each prayer, with each moment of reflection, I felt a renewed commitment to use my wealth in a way that would reflect the values of Islam, values of honesty, humility, and compassion. For true success, I realized, is not measured by wealth alone but by the goodness one brings into the world, by the blessings one bestows upon others, by the impact one has upon the lives of those around them.

As my work continued to flourish, I found myself increasingly aware of the role that humility played in guiding each decision, each interaction, each choice I made. Humility, as I had come to understand, was not a sign of weakness but a strength, a quiet assurance that success, when pursued with grace, becomes more than a personal achievement. It becomes a blessing, a gift that enriches not only one's life but the lives of others. I understood that the growth of my app, the wealth it had begun to yield, was not a reward for my efforts alone but a trust, a responsibility to use these blessings in a way that would bring goodness, a way that would honor both my family and my faith.

Each day, I felt a renewed sense of gratitude, a knowledge that my journey, though filled with challenges, was one that was blessed, a path that allowed me to serve, to contribute, to build something meaningful. In moments of success, when the app reached new milestones, when the user base continued to grow, I felt a quiet joy, a satisfaction that came not from wealth alone but from the knowledge that my work was making a difference, that it was bringing value, that it was fulfilling a purpose that went beyond personal ambition.

In moments of reflection, I felt a renewed commitment to remain grounded, to ensure that my work would continue to reflect the values of honesty, integrity, and service that had guided me from the beginning. For true success, I realized, is not a destination but a journey, a path that requires both patience and humility, a commitment to stay true to one's principles, a reminder that every blessing, every moment of success, is a gift, an opportunity to bring goodness into the world.

With each step forward, I found myself drawn closer to my faith, to the teachings that had been instilled within me since childhood, teachings that spoke of patience, of gratitude, of using one's blessings in a way that would bring honor to Allah. My app, I understood, was more than a product; it was a reflection of my journey, a testament to the values that had shaped my life, a platform that had the power to bring value, to serve, to uplift. And as I embraced this understanding, I felt a renewed sense of purpose, a commitment to use my work in a way that would honor both my ambitions and my faith, a way that would bring blessings upon all those who used it.

In moments of doubt, when the challenges seemed overwhelming, I would turn to prayer, seeking guidance, strength, and understanding, a reminder that my journey was not mine alone but a path that had been set for me, a journey that required both resilience and humility, a journey that would bring both success and blessings, a journey that would reflect the values of Islam. And as I prayed, I felt a peace, a quiet assurance that my work, though filled with challenges, was one that was blessed, a gift that allowed me to grow, to learn, to build a platform that would bring both success and purpose.

For in each challenge, in each moment of struggle, I saw a reminder that true success is measured not by wealth alone but by the impact one has upon the lives of others, by the goodness one brings into the world, by the blessings one bestows upon those who walk this journey with us.

The lessons of resilience, of gratitude, of humility became pillars that upheld my work, principles that reminded me that every step forward was a chance to honor both my ambitions and my faith. With each success, I felt a quiet joy, a satisfaction that came not from the wealth that my app had begun to yield but from the knowledge that my journey was making a difference, that it was bringing value, that it was fulfilling a purpose that went beyond personal ambition.

I began to see that my work was a means of service, a way to contribute, to use my blessings in a way that would bring goodness, that would reflect the values of Islam, values of honesty, humility, and compassion. This understanding filled me with a sense of responsibility, a commitment to ensure that my platform would continue to bring blessings upon all those who used it, to use my talents, my efforts, in a way that would honor both my family and my faith.

Each day, as I worked, as I crafted each feature, each function, I felt a renewed sense of purpose, a belief that my journey, though challenging, was one that was blessed, a path that would allow me to grow, to serve, to build something that would bring both profit and purpose, a platform that would reflect the goodness of Allah and the legacy of my family. For in each decision, in each action, I saw a reminder that my work was not mine alone but a shared vision, a reflection of the values that had shaped my life, values of honesty, humility, and service.

As the app continued to grow, so too did the opportunities to give back, to support those who were less fortunate, to use my blessings in a way that would bring goodness into the lives of others. I felt a deep sense of gratitude, a knowledge that my journey, though filled with challenges, was one that was blessed, a gift that allowed me to serve, to contribute, to build something meaningful. Each day became an opportunity, a chance to honor both my family and my faith, to use my talents, my efforts, in a way that would bring both success and blessings, a platform that would bring value into the lives of others.

The wealth that my work had begun to yield was not merely a treasure to be kept but a gift to be shared, a blessing that could bring joy, that could fulfill dreams, that could support those who were less fortunate. And as I embraced this understanding, I felt a renewed sense of purpose, a commitment to use my blessings in a way that would honor both my ambitions and my faith, a way that would bring blessings upon all those who walked this journey with me, a journey that was as much about serving others as it was about achieving personal success.

With each prayer, with each moment of reflection, I felt a renewed commitment to use my wealth in a way that would reflect the values of Islam, values of honesty, humility, and compassion. For true success, I realized, is not measured by wealth alone but by the goodness one brings into the world, by the blessings one bestows upon others, by the impact one has upon the lives of those around them.

In the presence of these blessings, I often found myself reflecting on the nature of intention, on the quiet power of purpose that had carried me through moments of doubt, moments of challenge, moments of growth. Intention, as I had come to understand, was not a single decision but a constant practice, a commitment to align one's actions, one's choices, with the values that had shaped one's life. Each day, as I worked, as I crafted each feature, each function, I reminded myself of the intention that had guided me from the beginning—a desire to build something meaningful, something that would honor both my ambitions and my faith.

In moments of reflection, I felt a renewed sense of purpose, a knowledge that my journey, though filled with challenges, was one that was blessed, a gift that allowed me to grow, to learn, to build something that would bring both profit and purpose, a platform that would reflect the values of Islam and the legacy of my family. For in each choice, in each action, I saw a reflection of the journey that had brought me to this point, a journey that had been filled with lessons, with moments of growth, with reminders that true success is not a treasure measured in coins but a legacy of kindness, of compassion, of service.

And as I embraced this purpose, I felt a renewed sense of dedication, a belief that my journey, though challenging, was one that was blessed, a path that allowed me to grow, to serve, to build a life that would bring both success and blessings upon all those who walked it with me.

The fruits of success, I discovered, are best shared, best savored in the presence of those who had believed in me from the beginning. My family, my friends, my mentors had all played a role in this journey, a journey that was as much theirs as it was mine. In the quiet moments of reflection, I would often find myself expressing gratitude, a gratitude that was as much for their support as it was for their guidance, their encouragement, their unwavering faith in my vision.

In their presence, I felt a quiet peace, a reminder that success, in its truest form, is a shared joy, a blessing that grows when it is given, a gift that brings not only wealth but meaning, fulfillment, a sense of purpose that goes beyond profit, beyond achievement. And as I looked upon my family, my friends, I felt a renewed commitment, a belief that my journey, though challenging, was one that was blessed, a path that would allow me to continue to grow, to serve, to build a life that would bring both success and blessings upon all those who walked it with me.

With each step forward, I felt a quiet joy, a satisfaction that came not from wealth alone but from the knowledge that my journey was making a difference, that it was bringing value, that it was fulfilling a purpose that went beyond personal ambition.

CHAPTER 7: A FATHER'S WISDOM

In a quiet evening after a long day's work, I found myself seated beside my father, seeking the wisdom that his years had gathered, the insights that had shaped his life. My father, a man of simple means but immeasurable depth, began to speak, sharing with me the values he had held dear, the principles that had carried him through life's hardships, the beliefs that had formed the foundation of our family's legacy. In his voice, I heard the strength of a man who had faced adversity, a man whose journey had been filled with both struggle and grace, a man who saw wealth not as a measure of success but as a trust, a responsibility to be handled with humility.

"My son," he began, his voice filled with a quiet conviction, "true wealth is not found in coins or treasures but in the heart, in the way a person lives, in the goodness he brings to others." His words were simple, yet they carried a profound wisdom, a reminder that my journey, though filled with ambition, was also a path of service, a chance to honor both my family and my faith.

In that conversation, I felt a deep sense of gratitude, a knowledge that my father's wisdom was a blessing, a guide that would carry me forward, a reminder that every blessing, every moment of success, was a gift, an opportunity to bring goodness into the world.

As we continued to speak, my father shared with me his understanding of wealth, a perspective that was as humbling as it was enlightening. "Wealth, my son, is not a reward but a test," he said, his eyes reflecting a depth of understanding that only comes from years of experience. "It is a trust that Allah has placed in our hands, a responsibility that must be used wisely, for the benefit of others, for the betterment of the community, for the blessings it can bring to those in need."

In those words, I found a new understanding of my journey, a reminder that my success was not mine alone but a gift that carried with it a responsibility, a duty to use my blessings in a way that would bring honor to Allah, that would uplift those who were less fortunate, that would contribute to a legacy of kindness, of compassion, of service. Each word my father spoke felt like a reminder, a call to approach my work with humility, with a heart that was open, that saw wealth not as a measure of worth but as a means of fulfilling a greater purpose.

With each moment, I felt a renewed commitment to ensure that my journey, though filled with challenges, would remain aligned with the values that my father had instilled within me, values of honesty, humility, and service.

As I sat beside my father, listening to his words, I began to see him in a new light, to recognize the depth of his humility, the quiet dignity with which he carried himself, a dignity that was not defined by wealth but by character, by strength, by resilience. My father, though a man of humble means, was a man of immeasurable wealth in spirit, a man whose life had been a testament to the values he held dear, a man whose legacy was not measured in coins but in kindness, in the goodness he had brought into the world.

In that moment, I realized that my father was a "poor dad" in wealth but rich in wisdom, a man who saw life not as a pursuit of riches but as a journey of integrity, a path that required both resilience and humility, a commitment to live in a way that honored both one's family and one's faith. I felt a deep sense of gratitude for his teachings, a knowledge that my journey, though filled with ambition, was also a path that would require humility, a reminder that true success is not found in wealth alone but in the goodness one brings into the lives of others.

And as I embraced this understanding, I felt a renewed commitment to live in a way that would honor my father's legacy, a way that would bring blessings upon all those who walked this journey with me.

One of the most profound lessons my father shared with me that evening was the importance of humility, a quality that he held dear, a value that he believed was the true measure of a person's worth. "My son," he said, "wealth does not define a person, nor does it elevate his status. A man's worth is measured not by his riches but by his character, by his honesty, his kindness, his compassion for those around him."

In those words, I felt a reminder of the values that had guided my father's life, a life that had been filled with challenges yet was marked by a quiet dignity, a strength that came not from wealth but from integrity, from a commitment to live in a way that honored both family and faith. Each word he spoke was a reminder that my journey, though filled with ambition, would require both humility and grace, a commitment to stay grounded, to remain true to the principles of honesty, of humility, of compassion.

With each lesson, I felt a renewed commitment to ensure that my work, my journey, would reflect these values, a reminder that true success is not measured by wealth alone but by the impact one has upon the lives of others, by the blessings one brings into the world, by the legacy of kindness, of compassion, of service.

In our conversation, my father spoke of the importance of integrity, a quality that he believed was the foundation of a life well-lived, a value that was essential in both personal and professional relationships. "Be honest, my son, in all your dealings," he said, his voice filled with a quiet strength, a reminder of the principles that had guided his life. "Let your word be your bond, let your actions reflect your values, let your work be a testament to your integrity."

His words resonated deeply within me, a reminder that my journey, though filled with ambition, was also a path that would require honesty, a commitment to ensure that my work would reflect the values of Islam, values of honesty, humility, and service. Each day, as I continued to build my platform, I reminded myself of my father's words, a call to approach each task with a heart that was both open and sincere, a heart that sought to build a business that was both profitable and ethical, a platform that would bring blessings upon all those who used it.

In moments of doubt, when the challenges seemed overwhelming, I would remember my father's advice, a reminder that true success is measured not by wealth alone but by the integrity one brings into one's work, by the honesty that defines each interaction, by the commitment to build something that is both valuable and meaningful.

As we continued to speak, my father shared with me the importance of giving back, of using one's blessings in a way that would bring goodness into the lives of others, a way that would support those who were less fortunate, a way that would honor both one's family and one's faith. "Wealth is a gift, my son, a blessing that carries with it the responsibility to help, to uplift, to bring joy to those in need."

In those words, I felt a renewed understanding of my journey, a reminder that my success was not mine alone but a trust, a gift that I had been granted, a chance to use my wealth in a way that would bring blessings upon all those who walked this journey with me. Each day became an opportunity, a chance to give, to support, to contribute to something greater, to build a legacy of kindness, of compassion, of service.

For in each blessing, I saw a reminder that true success is measured not by the coins in one's hand but by the goodness in one's heart, by the impact one has upon the lives of others, by the blessings one bestows upon those who are less fortunate.

As the evening continued, my father shared with me his views on responsibility, a concept that he believed was central to any form of success, a value that went beyond mere duty. "Responsibility, my son," he said, "is not merely about doing what is expected, but about going beyond, about ensuring that every action, every choice, is aligned with integrity and respect." His words carried a weight, a gravity that only comes from years of living by one's principles, a reminder that true success requires not only ambition but accountability, a dedication to uphold the trust that others place in us.

In my father's understanding, responsibility extended beyond one's immediate circle; it encompassed one's community, one's faith, one's duty to use blessings wisely and honorably. He spoke of responsibility as a calling, a charge given to each person to act in a way that reflects the values of humility, compassion, and service. And as I listened, I felt a renewed sense of commitment, a desire to ensure that my journey, though filled with ambition, would remain grounded in these values, that each choice I made would be a testament to my dedication to live by the principles my father had instilled within me.

In moments of doubt, when the challenges felt overwhelming, I would remember my father's words, a reminder that my journey, though personal, was also a path that allowed me to contribute to something greater, a chance to build a life that would bring both success and honor, a life that would reflect the values of Islam, values of honesty, humility, and service.

My father continued to share with me his thoughts on resilience, a quality that he held in high regard, a strength that he believed was essential for any journey, for any path that sought to achieve greatness. "Resilience, my son," he said, "is the ability to rise again and again, to face each challenge with a heart that does not waver, a spirit that believes in the goodness of the journey, no matter how difficult the road may seem." His voice carried a quiet strength, a reminder that life, with all its trials and tribulations, is a test, a path that requires both patience and perseverance.

As he spoke, I felt a renewed sense of purpose, a belief that my journey, though filled with obstacles, was one that would require both resilience and faith, a commitment to continue, to strive, to work toward a life that would bring both success and blessings upon all those who walked it with me. In my father's words, I found a reminder of the importance of resilience, a call to approach each challenge with a heart that was both humble and determined, a heart that trusted in Allah's plan, a heart that believed in the goodness of the journey.

With each lesson, I felt a deep sense of gratitude, a knowledge that my journey, though challenging, was one that was blessed, a path that allowed me to grow, to learn, to build something that would bring both profit and purpose, a platform that would honor both my ambitions and my faith.

In the quiet moments of our conversation, my father shared with me his understanding of balance, a quality that he believed was essential in both personal and professional life, a value that required both discipline and discernment. "My son," he said, "life is a journey that requires balance, a path that requires us to honor both our ambitions and our responsibilities, to ensure that each step we take is aligned with the values that have shaped our lives."

In his words, I found a reminder of the importance of balance, a call to approach each decision with a heart that was both discerning and humble, a heart that sought to build a business that was both profitable and meaningful, a business that would bring blessings upon all those who used it. Balance, as my father understood it, was not merely about achieving harmony but about living with intention, about ensuring that each choice, each action, reflected the values of honesty, integrity, and compassion that had guided him.

With each lesson, I felt a renewed sense of purpose, a commitment to live in a way that would honor both my family and my faith, a reminder that true success is not measured by wealth alone but by the goodness one brings into the lives of others, by the blessings one bestows upon those who walk this journey with us.

Our conversation turned to the concept of generosity, a value that my father believed was not merely an act but a way of life, a practice that brought blessings upon both the giver and the receiver. "Generosity, my son," he said, "is the ability to give without expecting in return, a reminder that wealth, when shared, becomes a blessing, a gift that enriches not only the one who receives but the one who gives." His words carried a profound wisdom, a reminder that true wealth is not measured by the coins in one's hand but by the goodness in one's heart, by the kindness one bestows upon those who are less fortunate.

In those words, I felt a renewed understanding of my journey, a reminder that my success was not mine alone but a trust, a gift that I had been granted, a chance to use my blessings in a way that would bring goodness into the lives of others. Each day became an opportunity, a chance to give, to support, to contribute to something greater, to build a legacy of kindness, of compassion, of service. For in each blessing, I saw a reminder that true success is measured not by wealth alone but by the impact one has upon the lives of others, by the blessings one brings into the world.

With each prayer, with each moment of reflection, I felt a renewed commitment to use my wealth in a way that would reflect the values of Islam, values of honesty, humility, and compassion, a commitment to build a life that would bring both success and honor, a life that would reflect the goodness of Allah and the legacy of my family.

As our conversation drew to a close, my father shared with me one final lesson, a lesson that was as humbling as it was profound—a reminder of the impermanence of wealth, of the fleeting nature of success, a call to live in a way that honored both one's family and one's faith. "Remember, my son," he said, "wealth is but a passing gift, a treasure that can be taken as quickly as it is given. True wealth lies not in riches but in the legacy one leaves, in the kindness one bestows, in the goodness one brings into the lives of others."

In those words, I found a renewed understanding of my journey, a reminder that my success, though valuable, was also temporary, a gift that carried with it a responsibility to live in a way that would bring blessings upon those around me, a way that would honor both my ambitions and my faith. For in each blessing, I saw a reminder that true success is not measured by wealth alone but by the legacy of kindness, of compassion, of service that one leaves behind.

In that moment, I felt a deep sense of gratitude for my father's wisdom, a knowledge that my journey, though filled with ambition, was also a path of service, a chance to build a life that would bring both success and blessings upon all those who walked it with me.

In the days that followed our conversation, I found myself reflecting upon my father's words, upon the lessons he had shared, upon the wisdom that had been instilled within me. Each word felt like a reminder, a call to approach my work with humility, with a heart that was both open and sincere, a heart that sought to build a business that was both profitable and meaningful, a platform that would bring blessings upon all those who used it.

With each lesson, I felt a renewed commitment to ensure that my journey, though filled with challenges, would remain aligned with the values that my father had instilled within me, values of honesty, humility, and service. For true success, I realized, is not a destination but a journey, a path that requires both patience and humility, a commitment to stay grounded, to remain true to the principles of honesty, integrity, and compassion that had guided me from the beginning.

In moments of doubt, when the challenges seemed overwhelming, I would remember my father's wisdom, a reminder that my journey was guided not by my own strength but by the blessings of Allah, by a wisdom that was leading me to a life that would bring both success and honor, a life that would reflect the values of Islam, values of honesty, humility, and compassion.

As the weeks went on, my father's words lingered within me, like a compass pointing me toward the deeper truths that lay beneath the surface of success. One evening, he spoke of legacy—not as an inheritance of wealth but as an inheritance of values, of character, of the goodness one leaves behind. "My son," he began, his voice quiet yet steady, "a legacy is not something that is measured in riches or possessions; it is the kindness one spreads, the values one upholds, the love one shows to those around him."

In those words, I felt a reminder of the importance of living in a way that would honor both one's family and one's faith, a reminder that true success is not measured by wealth alone but by the impact one has upon the lives of others, by the blessings one brings into the world. My father's understanding of legacy was a call to live with intention, to approach each day as an opportunity to bring goodness, to uplift, to serve. His words carried a weight that resonated deeply within me, a call to ensure that my journey, though personal, would remain aligned with the values that he had instilled within me.

With each lesson, I felt a renewed sense of purpose, a commitment to live in a way that would honor my father's legacy, a way that would bring blessings upon all those who walked this journey with me.

My father's lessons on humility became a constant reminder as my work grew, as my app reached new heights, as my platform continued to expand. He would often say, "Humility, my son, is not merely about thinking less of oneself, but about placing others before oneself, about using one's blessings in a way that brings joy, that uplifts, that serves." His understanding of humility was profound, a quality that was not about diminishing oneself but about elevating others, about ensuring that one's success did not create distance but fostered connection, about using one's position to serve, to contribute, to bring value into the lives of those around him.

In moments of success, when the wealth my work had begun to yield became tangible, I felt a renewed commitment to approach each step with humility, a reminder that my journey, though rewarding, was also a path of service, a path that required both humility and grace, a commitment to live in a way that would bring blessings upon those who placed their trust in me. For in each blessing, I saw a reminder of the values that had guided my father's life, values of honesty, humility, and compassion, a call to build a business that was not only profitable but meaningful, a business that would reflect the goodness of Allah and the legacy of my family.

With each moment of reflection, I felt a renewed commitment to use my wealth in a way that would bring goodness into the world, a way that would honor both my ambitions and my faith.

In one of our last conversations, my father shared with me a story from his youth, a time when he had faced hardship, a time when he had learned the value of perseverance, of resilience, of a heart that did not waver in the face of adversity. "My son," he began, "life will test you in ways you cannot foresee, in ways that will challenge every value, every belief you hold dear. But remember, strength is not found in the absence of struggle but in the way one rises, the way one faces each challenge with a heart that is both strong and humble."

His story was a reminder that resilience was not merely a quality but a practice, a commitment to rise again and again, to face each challenge with a heart that believed in the goodness of the journey, a spirit that trusted in Allah's plan, a soul that found strength in the values that had been instilled within it. In his words, I found a reminder of the importance of resilience, a call to approach each challenge with a heart that was both open and strong, a heart that believed that every struggle, every obstacle, was a lesson, a chance to grow, to learn, to build a life that would bring both success and blessings.

With each lesson, I felt a renewed commitment to live in a way that would honor my father's legacy, a way that would bring blessings upon all those who walked this journey with me.

As I continued to build upon my work, to expand my platform, I carried with me the teachings of my father, the wisdom that had shaped his life, the values that he had instilled within me. His lessons on humility, resilience, integrity, and generosity became a foundation upon which I built my journey, a reminder that true success is not measured by wealth alone but by the impact one has upon the lives of others, by the blessings one brings into the world, by the legacy one leaves behind.

In the quiet moments of reflection, I would often find myself returning to my father's words, to the lessons he had shared, to the wisdom that had been passed down from generation to generation, a wisdom that was as timeless as it was profound. Each word felt like a call to approach my work with humility, with a heart that was both open and sincere, a heart that sought to build a business that was both profitable and meaningful, a platform that would bring blessings upon all those who used it.

With each step forward, I felt a deep sense of gratitude for my father's wisdom, a knowledge that my journey, though personal, was also a path of service, a path that required both humility and grace, a commitment to live in a way that would bring blessings upon all those who walked this journey with me, a way that would honor both my ambitions and my faith, a way that would reflect the goodness of Allah and the legacy of my family.

CHAPTER 8: BUILDING A DREAM

As the dawn of new beginnings filled the sky, I awoke with a resolve strengthened by the wisdom of my father and the guidance of my faith. This was a fresh start, a renewed chapter, and a deeper dedication to my app—my venture that, in many ways, mirrored my own journey. With each line of code, each feature refined, I felt as though I were piecing together parts of myself, bringing to life a vision that held purpose, service, and meaning. The goal was no longer simply to create a profitable business; it was to craft a tool that would serve, that would offer value, that would uphold the principles I cherished.

This focus lent a new clarity to my work. I began each day with a prayer, asking for guidance and strength, with a heart that sought not only success but blessings for those who would use my app. With renewed energy, I spent hours working, the world around me fading as I dove deeper into this labor of love. For as my app took shape, I felt a profound connection to the journey, to the purpose that was much greater than myself. In those moments, the pursuit of wealth faded in the background, giving way to a sense of purpose, a joy that was deeply fulfilling.

With this resolve, I committed myself to the path that lay ahead, ready to face each challenge, to refine each detail, to build a dream that would honor both my ambitions and my faith.

As the days passed, I focused on refining the app based on the feedback I received, the insights that flowed in from users who trusted my work, who believed in the vision that had driven me from the beginning. This feedback was invaluable, a gift that offered me a glimpse into the hearts and minds of those who used my app, who had placed their trust in my platform. Each suggestion, each request was a reminder of the importance of quality, a call to ensure that every feature, every detail, was crafted with care, with a dedication to excellence.

The process of refining the app became a journey in itself, a path that required both patience and humility, a commitment to listen, to learn, to adapt. I spent hours reviewing each comment, each insight, seeking ways to improve, to enhance, to build a product that would not only meet expectations but exceed them. For in each adjustment, in each improvement, I saw a reflection of my own growth, a testament to the values that had shaped my life, values of honesty, integrity, and compassion.

With each update, I felt a renewed sense of purpose, a commitment to ensure that my work would continue to bring value, to serve, to uplift, to fulfill the purpose that had guided me from the beginning.

As my app grew, so too did the need to build a user base, to reach a wider audience, to bring my work to those who could benefit from its features. I began to explore the world of marketing, learning the intricacies of promotion, the strategies that would allow me to reach potential users, to share my vision with those who might find value in my platform. Each day, I crafted campaigns, designed visuals, wrote messages that conveyed the heart of my work, the purpose that had driven me, the service that my app offered.

The process of building a user base was both exciting and challenging, a journey that required both resilience and dedication, a commitment to share my vision in a way that resonated, that connected, that invited others to join me on this path. I saw a steady increase in downloads, each new user a testament to the impact my work was having, a reminder that my journey, though filled with challenges, was one that was blessed, a gift that allowed me to serve, to contribute, to build something meaningful.

With each new user, each new download, I felt a sense of gratitude, a knowledge that my journey, though personal, was also a path that allowed me to connect, to build a community, to bring blessings upon all those who walked this journey with me.

In the process of building this user base, I began to understand the true value of quality, the importance of creating a product that was well-crafted, that was designed with care, that offered not only functionality but an experience. I realized that quick fixes, shortcuts, compromises would not serve my purpose, that a well-made product was one that would stand the test of time, one that would attract users not by gimmicks but by genuine value, by a dedication to excellence, by a commitment to quality.

Each feature, each function became an opportunity to refine, to improve, to build something that would honor both my ambitions and my faith, something that would bring blessings upon all those who used it. I felt a renewed commitment to ensure that my work, my app, would be a reflection of the values that had guided me, values of honesty, integrity, and compassion. For in each line of code, in each detail, I saw a reflection of my own journey, a reminder that true success is measured not by wealth alone but by the impact one has upon the lives of others.

With each improvement, I felt a renewed sense of purpose, a commitment to build something that was both profitable and meaningful, a platform that would bring blessings upon all those who used it.

Throughout this journey, I found myself leaning on the support of my friends Aman and Maqsood, brothers who had walked this path with me, who had believed in my vision, who had offered their insights, their support, their encouragement. Aman, with his knack for marketing, helped me craft campaigns that resonated, messages that conveyed the heart of my work, strategies that would allow my app to reach those who could benefit from it. Maqsood, with his technical expertise, provided guidance, insights, suggestions that improved the functionality of the app, that ensured each feature, each function, was crafted with care.

Together, we worked, each of us contributing our strengths, each of us bringing our unique skills, each of us dedicated to building something that was valuable, meaningful, a product that would honor both our ambitions and our values. The process of working together strengthened our friendship, deepened our bond, reminded us of the importance of community, of the power of shared vision, of the blessings that come from collaboration.

With each day, I felt a renewed sense of gratitude for their support, a reminder that my journey, though personal, was one that was shared, a path that allowed me to build something that would bring blessings upon all those who walked it with me.

As the work continued, I found myself stepping into a new role, a role that required not only technical skill but leadership, a quality that I had begun to cultivate, a strength that was as much about humility as it was about confidence. I learned to delegate tasks, to trust my friends, to allow each member of my team to bring their expertise, their insights, their strengths to the table. Leadership, I realized, was not about control but about guidance, about creating a space where each person could contribute, where each voice was valued, where each effort was acknowledged.

In this role, I felt a renewed sense of responsibility, a commitment to build a team that was grounded in the values that had shaped my journey, values of honesty, humility, and compassion. I understood that leadership was as much about service as it was about direction, a call to build a team that would bring blessings upon all those who walked this journey with me.

With each day, I felt a renewed sense of purpose, a knowledge that my journey, though filled with challenges, was one that was blessed, a path that allowed me to grow, to learn, to build something that would bring both success and blessings, a reminder that true success is measured not by wealth alone but by the legacy one leaves behind.

As I delved deeper into the process of building my app, I realized that each line of code, each feature refined, was more than just a task; it was a manifestation of my vision, a step closer to creating something that would bring value to others. Every morning, as I sat at my desk, I felt a renewed commitment to ensure that my work would be more than functional—it would be meaningful, intuitive, a tool that would serve with grace and purpose. I came to understand that the true power of technology lies not just in its capacity to achieve but in its ability to connect, to offer a solution that could improve lives, even in the smallest of ways.

The technical side of my work was a challenge I embraced wholeheartedly. I found myself learning new skills, discovering shortcuts, refining processes, diving into resources that expanded my understanding of programming and user experience. There were nights when I spent hours solving a single bug, moments when I felt the frustration of hitting a wall, yet with each solution, each breakthrough, I felt a quiet pride, a sense of growth, a belief that every challenge was a step forward, a chance to refine my craft, to build something that would truly serve others.

In these moments of focus, I felt a deep sense of purpose, a commitment to ensure that my work would reflect the values that had guided me from the beginning, values of integrity, of quality, of a dedication to excellence.

As my platform continued to expand, so too did my understanding of what it meant to build a community, to cultivate a user base that was not just transactional but engaged, connected, invested in the vision I held. I began to see each user as a part of a larger whole, as individuals who were not merely customers but participants in this journey, supporters who believed in the purpose that my app offered. This realization transformed my approach to customer service, to user interaction, to the way I responded to feedback and inquiries.

I set up a channel where users could reach out directly, a platform for them to share their experiences, their suggestions, their challenges. I read through each message, each piece of feedback, with a heart that was open, a heart that saw these words not as mere requests but as gifts, as opportunities to learn, to improve, to build something that would truly resonate. I engaged with each user personally, responding with gratitude, with a desire to understand, to connect, to ensure that their experience with my app was positive, meaningful, a reflection of the values that had shaped my journey.

With each interaction, I felt a renewed sense of gratitude, a knowledge that my journey, though personal, was also a path that allowed me to build a community, to connect with those who believed in my vision, to bring blessings upon all those who walked this journey with me.

As the weeks turned into months, I began to see the impact of my work, the way in which my app was making a difference, the way it was reaching people, serving them, meeting their needs. This impact was a reminder of the blessings that Allah had granted me, a reminder that my journey, though challenging, was one that was blessed, a gift that allowed me to serve, to contribute, to build something meaningful. Each day became an opportunity, a chance to improve, to refine, to ensure that my work would remain a source of value, a platform that would bring blessings upon all those who used it.

In these moments of reflection, I felt a deep sense of gratitude, a knowledge that my journey, though personal, was also a path that allowed me to serve, to uplift, to build something that would honor both my ambitions and my faith. For true success, I realized, was not a destination but a journey, a path that requires both patience and resilience, a commitment to stay grounded, to remain true to one's values, a reminder that every blessing, every moment of success, is a gift, an opportunity to bring goodness into the world.

With each day, I felt a renewed sense of purpose, a commitment to build a platform that would bring both profit and purpose, a reminder that true wealth is measured not by the coins in one's hand but by the goodness in one's heart, by the impact one has upon the lives of others.

The journey of building this app was one that transformed not only my skills but my character, teaching me lessons of patience, resilience, humility, and service. Each step, each challenge was a reminder that success is not merely about achieving goals but about growing, learning, becoming a person who is capable of carrying the responsibilities that come with blessings. I began to see my work as a reflection of my journey, a testament to the values that had shaped my life, values of honesty, humility, and compassion.

As the user base continued to grow, I found myself increasingly aware of the importance of staying grounded, of ensuring that each success, each milestone, was met with gratitude, with a commitment to remain true to the purpose that had driven me from the beginning. I reminded myself that true success is not measured by wealth alone but by the legacy one leaves, by the goodness one brings into the lives of others, by the blessings one bestows upon those who walk this journey with us.

In moments of reflection, I felt a renewed commitment to ensure that my work would continue to reflect these values, a reminder that my journey, though filled with challenges, was one that was blessed, a gift that allowed me to grow, to serve, to build something meaningful, a platform that would bring blessings upon all those who used it.

As I looked upon the journey I had walked, I felt a deep sense of gratitude for the support, the guidance, the encouragement of those who had believed in me, who had supported my vision, who had offered their insights, their expertise, their time. My friends Aman and Maqsood had been instrumental in this journey, their belief in my vision a source of strength, a reminder that my journey, though personal, was also a shared vision, a path that allowed us to work together, to build something that was valuable, meaningful, a reflection of the values we held dear.

Together, we celebrated each success, each milestone, each achievement with gratitude, with a commitment to remain humble, to ensure that our work would continue to bring value, to serve, to uplift, to honor both our ambitions and our values. In their presence, I felt a sense of joy, a reminder that true success is a shared journey, a blessing that grows when it is given, a gift that brings not only wealth but meaning, fulfillment, a sense of purpose that goes beyond profit, beyond achievement.

With each moment of reflection, I felt a renewed commitment to use my blessings in a way that would honor both my family and my faith, a way that would bring blessings upon all those who walked this journey with me, a journey that was as much about serving others as it was about achieving personal success.

As my work gained traction and the app began to garner attention, I found myself facing new challenges, opportunities that required both discernment and integrity, choices that tested my commitment to the values that had guided me. There were moments when shortcuts, compromises, easy paths presented themselves, yet I reminded myself that true success is built on a foundation of honesty, of integrity, of a commitment to uphold one's principles even in the face of temptation.

With each decision, I felt a renewed sense of responsibility, a reminder that my journey, though filled with ambition, was also a path that required humility, a commitment to stay grounded, to remain true to the values that had shaped my journey, values of honesty, humility, and compassion. For true success, I realized, is not merely about achieving one's goals but about doing so in a way that honors one's principles, a way that brings blessings upon all those who walk this journey with us.

In these moments of choice, I felt a deep sense of gratitude for the lessons I had learned, a knowledge that my journey, though personal, was also a path that allowed me to build a life that would bring both success and blessings, a life that would honor both my ambitions and my faith.

In the quiet of the evening, as I reviewed the progress of my app, I found myself contemplating the role it had begun to play in the lives of those who used it. I received messages from users sharing how the app had made their day simpler, helped them save time, or allowed them to connect with resources they valued. Each message was a reminder that my work was not just a collection of features or functions; it was a service, a means of bringing ease, a reflection of the values of compassion and service that had guided me from the beginning. In those moments, I felt a deep sense of gratitude, a knowledge that my journey, though challenging, was one that was blessed, a path that allowed me to bring goodness into the world.

The app was a small piece of technology, yet in each interaction, I saw its potential to impact lives, to serve, to offer a service that was valuable and meaningful. This realization humbled me, reminding me that each step forward was a chance to improve, to refine, to ensure that my work would continue to be a source of blessings. I became dedicated to making each user's experience a positive one, crafting every aspect of the app with care, with an intention to serve, with a commitment to excellence.

For in each feature, I saw a reminder that true success is not measured by the number of downloads alone but by the value one brings into the lives of others, by the kindness one extends, by the blessings one bestows upon those who trust in one's work.

The journey of building this platform was one that required both resilience and adaptability, qualities that had become as essential to my work as the technical skills I had cultivated. Each new update, each improvement, was an opportunity to refine, to respond to the needs of my users, to adapt to the feedback that flowed in. I came to see feedback as a gift, a chance to learn, to grow, to build something that would truly resonate with those who used it. Each comment, each suggestion became a part of my journey, a part of the evolution of my app, a reminder that true success is measured not by wealth alone but by the willingness to listen, to learn, to grow.

In those moments, I felt a renewed sense of commitment to my users, a knowledge that my journey, though personal, was also a path that allowed me to connect, to build relationships, to create a platform that was both valuable and meaningful. Each user became a part of my journey, a reminder of the purpose that had driven me from the beginning, a purpose that was as much about serving others as it was about achieving success.

With each update, I felt a deep sense of gratitude for the trust that my users had placed in me, a reminder that my work, though challenging, was also a blessing, a chance to build something that would bring both success and blessings upon all those who used it.

As the app continued to gain traction, I found myself thinking of ways to expand its reach, to build a network that would bring value to even more users, to create a community that was united by a shared vision, a shared purpose, a shared commitment to excellence. The process of building this community was both exciting and humbling, a journey that required both patience and perseverance, a dedication to sharing my work with those who might benefit from it, a commitment to ensuring that each interaction, each experience, was positive, meaningful, a reflection of the values that had shaped my journey.

I reached out to influencers, to content creators, to those who believed in my vision, who saw the potential of my app, who were willing to share it with their audiences, to introduce it to those who could find value in its features. Each collaboration, each partnership was a reminder of the importance of community, a reminder that my journey, though personal, was also a path that allowed me to connect, to build relationships, to create a platform that was both valuable and meaningful.

With each step forward, I felt a renewed sense of purpose, a commitment to build a community that would bring blessings upon all those who walked this journey with me, a community that would reflect the values of honesty, humility, and compassion.

In the process of building this community, I came to understand the power of storytelling, the importance of sharing my journey, my vision, my purpose in a way that resonated, that connected, that invited others to join me on this path. I began to share my story, to open up about the challenges I had faced, the lessons I had learned, the purpose that had driven me from the beginning. Each story, each message was a piece of my journey, a reflection of the values that had shaped my life, values of honesty, humility, and service.

Through this storytelling, I felt a sense of connection, a reminder that my journey, though personal, was also a path that allowed me to inspire, to uplift, to encourage those who might be walking similar paths, those who might be facing their own challenges, who might be seeking guidance, support, a reminder that they too could achieve, that they too could build something meaningful. In each story, I saw a reminder of the importance of authenticity, a call to approach each message with a heart that was both open and sincere, a heart that sought to share not only the successes but the struggles, the lessons, the growth that had defined my journey.

With each story, I felt a renewed commitment to use my voice in a way that would bring blessings upon those who heard it, a voice that would inspire, that would uplift, that would bring goodness into the lives of those who walked this journey with me.

As the community around my app grew, I found myself reflecting on the impact it was having, the way in which it was connecting people, the way in which it was fulfilling a purpose that went beyond profit, beyond personal gain. I began to see my work as a service, a means of contributing to something greater, a platform that offered value, that brought joy, that fulfilled needs in a way that was both ethical and meaningful. This understanding filled me with a sense of responsibility, a commitment to ensure that my work would continue to reflect the values that had guided me, values of honesty, humility, and compassion.

In moments of doubt, when the challenges felt overwhelming, I would remind myself of the purpose that had driven me from the beginning, a purpose that was as much about serving others as it was about achieving success. For in each feature, in each function, I saw a reminder of the journey that had brought me to this point, a journey that had been filled with lessons, with moments of growth, with reminders that true success is measured not by wealth alone but by the impact one has upon the lives of others.

With each day, I felt a renewed sense of purpose, a commitment to build a platform that would bring both profit and purpose, a reminder that true wealth is measured not by the coins in one's hand but by the goodness in one's heart, by the blessings one brings into the lives of others.

As I looked upon the journey I had walked, I felt a deep sense of gratitude for the blessings that had brought me here, for the support, the encouragement, the belief of those who had stood by me, who had offered their insights, their time, their friendship. In those moments, I felt a renewed commitment to use my work, my app, my journey, in a way that would bring blessings upon those who had trusted in my vision, who had walked this path with me, who had believed in the potential of my work.

With each reflection, I felt a renewed sense of gratitude for the lessons I had learned, a knowledge that my journey, though personal, was also a path that allowed me to build something that was valuable, meaningful, a reminder that true success is not measured by wealth alone but by the legacy of kindness, of compassion, of service that one leaves behind. For in each blessing, in each moment of success, I saw a reminder of the importance of humility, a call to live in a way that honored both my ambitions and my faith, a life that would bring blessings upon all those who walked this journey with me.

With each step forward, I felt a renewed commitment to use my blessings in a way that would honor both my family and my faith, a way that would reflect the goodness of Allah, a way that would bring goodness into the lives of others.

CHAPTER 9: THE ROAD TO SUCCESS

With my app growing in popularity, I found myself embracing the responsibilities that came with its success. The influx of new users brought both excitement and challenges, a reminder that success was as much about sustaining growth as it was about achieving it. I dedicated myself to refining each feature, ensuring that every aspect of the app aligned with the vision I had for it—a tool that would serve, simplify, and bring value to people's lives. Each day, as I monitored user feedback and assessed the app's performance, I realized the importance of consistency, the need to maintain the same level of excellence that had fueled its initial growth.

In the midst of this expansion, I worked tirelessly to keep the app's core purpose intact, to ensure that as it grew, it would remain a tool grounded in integrity, in quality, in a dedication to serve rather than merely profit. Managing this growth required both patience and resilience, qualities that had become essential in navigating the intricacies of scaling a platform. I found myself spending long hours refining processes, implementing improvements, ensuring that my app could sustain this growth without compromising its purpose.

With each effort, I felt a renewed sense of gratitude, a reminder that my journey, though filled with challenges, was also a path that allowed me to grow, to serve, to build something that would bring blessings upon all those who used it.

As the app's growth continued, I became increasingly aware of the importance of ethical decision-making. Each choice I faced, each direction I considered, had to align with my faith, with the values that had guided my journey from the beginning. In the world of business, it is easy to be tempted by shortcuts, to be lured by opportunities that promise quick gains yet stray from one's principles. Yet I reminded myself that true success is built on a foundation of honesty, of integrity, of a commitment to uphold one's values even in the face of temptation.

Each decision became a reflection of my dedication to my faith, a reminder that my journey, though personal, was also a testament to the values of Islam, values of honesty, humility, and service. In moments of choice, I would pause, seeking guidance, asking for strength, for the wisdom to make decisions that would honor both my ambitions and my beliefs. I understood that my work was not mine alone but a gift, a blessing that carried with it a responsibility to act with integrity, to ensure that each choice reflected the principles of honesty and humility.

With each decision, I felt a renewed sense of responsibility, a commitment to build a business that would bring blessings upon all those who walked this journey with me, a business that would reflect the values of Islam, values of honesty, humility, and compassion.

As the app continued to thrive, I found myself exploring new opportunities, avenues that would allow me to expand, to diversify, to build something that would bring both profit and purpose. Inspired by the success of my first app, I began working on a second idea, a platform that would complement my original app, that would offer additional value, that would allow me to reach a wider audience. The process of building this second app was as challenging as it was exciting, a journey that required both creativity and resilience, a dedication to refine, to improve, to build something that would honor both my ambitions and my values.

In these moments of creation, I felt a renewed sense of purpose, a belief that my journey, though filled with challenges, was one that was blessed, a path that allowed me to grow, to learn, to build something that would bring both success and blessings. For in each idea, in each new venture, I saw a reflection of the journey that had brought me to this point, a journey that had been filled with lessons, with moments of growth, with reminders that true success is measured not by wealth alone but by the impact one has upon the lives of others.

With each new venture, I felt a renewed sense of commitment to use my skills, my talents, in a way that would bring blessings upon all those who walked this journey with me, a way that would honor both my ambitions and my faith.

As my business ventures continued to grow, I found myself in a position to support my family, to give back to those who had sacrificed so much for me, to honor the legacy of love and dedication that my parents had instilled within me. My father, who had taught me the values of humility, of resilience, of honesty, became a source of inspiration, a reminder that my success, though valuable, was also a trust, a responsibility to use my blessings in a way that would honor both my family and my faith.

In moments of reflection, I felt a deep sense of gratitude for the sacrifices my parents had made, for the values they had instilled within me, for the lessons they had taught me, lessons that had become the foundation of my journey, the guiding principles that had shaped my path. With each blessing, with each success, I felt a renewed commitment to give back, to support my family, to ensure that my success would be a source of joy, of pride, of gratitude for those who had believed in me, who had supported my vision, who had offered their love, their encouragement, their belief in my potential.

For true success, I realized, is not measured by wealth alone but by the legacy one leaves, by the kindness one extends, by the blessings one brings into the lives of those who walk this journey with us.

Throughout this journey, I came to see the profound impact of my faith on every aspect of my business, a reminder that my beliefs, my values, were not separate from my work but an integral part of it, a foundation upon which each decision, each action, was built. My faith became a source of strength, a reminder that my journey, though challenging, was also a path that was blessed, a path that allowed me to serve, to contribute, to build something meaningful. Each prayer, each moment of reflection, was a reminder of the purpose that had driven me from the beginning, a purpose that was as much about serving others as it was about achieving success.

In moments of doubt, when the challenges felt overwhelming, I would turn to my faith, seeking guidance, strength, and reassurance, a reminder that my journey was not mine alone but a path that had been set for me, a journey that required both resilience and humility, a journey that would bring both success and blessings, a journey that would reflect the values of Islam.

With each step forward, I felt a renewed sense of purpose, a commitment to build a business that would bring blessings upon all those who walked this journey with me, a business that would honor both my ambitions and my faith, a business that would reflect the goodness of Allah and the values that had shaped my life.

As my business continued to grow, I found myself reaching out to mentors, to those who had walked this path before me, who had faced the same challenges, who understood the complexities of building a business that was both profitable and ethical. I connected with entrepreneurs who shared my values, who believed in the importance of integrity, of humility, of a commitment to build something that was valuable, meaningful, a reflection of the values of Islam. These mentors offered me guidance, insights, wisdom that became invaluable in navigating the intricacies of business, in making choices that would honor both my ambitions and my beliefs.

In their presence, I felt a renewed sense of purpose, a reminder that my journey, though personal, was also a shared vision, a path that allowed me to learn, to grow, to build something that would bring blessings upon all those who walked this journey with me. For true success, I realized, is not a solitary achievement but a shared journey, a blessing that grows when it is given, a gift that brings not only wealth but meaning, fulfillment, a sense of purpose that goes beyond profit, beyond achievement.

With each lesson, I felt a deep sense of gratitude for their guidance, a knowledge that my journey, though challenging, was one that was blessed, a path that allowed me to grow, to learn, to build something that would bring both success and blessings upon all those who used it.

As my business continued to grow, I found myself at a crossroad where new opportunities presented themselves daily. With this growth came the responsibility to choose wisely, to assess each path not only by its potential profitability but by its alignment with my values. Each decision, each step forward became a test of my commitment to remain grounded, to ensure that my journey stayed true to the purpose that had guided me from the start. I often reflected on my father's wisdom, the principles he had instilled within me, reminders that true success is measured not by the wealth one accumulates but by the goodness one brings into the world.

In moments of uncertainty, I would turn to prayer, asking for guidance, seeking the strength to make choices that would honor both my ambitions and my faith. These moments of reflection became an integral part of my journey, a reminder that my work was not mine alone but a path that had been entrusted to me, a responsibility to act with integrity, to ensure that every decision, every action reflected the values of Islam, values of honesty, humility, and service. With each choice, I felt a renewed commitment to stay true to this path, a path that would bring blessings upon all those who walked this journey with me.

With each moment of reflection, I felt a renewed sense of purpose, a commitment to build a business that would bring both success and blessings, a business that would honor both my ambitions and my values.

As the months passed, I began to consider the legacy I wished to leave, the impact I wanted my work to have, the values I wanted to reflect through my business. I understood that my journey, though personal, was also a means of contributing to something greater, a path that allowed me to serve, to uplift, to build a life that would bring both success and blessings upon those around me. Each step forward became an opportunity to refine, to improve, to ensure that my work would remain aligned with this purpose, a reminder that true success is not measured by wealth alone but by the legacy one leaves, by the kindness one bestows, by the blessings one brings into the lives of others.

With this understanding, I felt a renewed commitment to approach each day, each task, with a heart that was both humble and determined, a heart that sought to build a business that was valuable, meaningful, a reflection of the values that had guided me from the beginning. My work became a means of expressing gratitude, a chance to honor the blessings that had brought me here, a reminder that my journey, though challenging, was one that was blessed, a path that allowed me to bring goodness into the world, to build something that would bring blessings upon all those who used it.

For in each choice, in each action, I saw a reminder of the journey that had brought me to this point, a journey that had been filled with lessons, with moments of growth, with reminders that true success is measured not by wealth alone but by the impact one has upon the lives of others.

In the process of building my business, I came to understand the value of patience, a quality that had become as essential as the technical skills I had cultivated, a strength that allowed me to navigate the complexities of growth with a heart that was both calm and resilient. Patience, as I had learned, was not merely a matter of waiting but a practice of endurance, a commitment to trust in the process, to believe in the goodness of the journey even in the face of challenges, even when progress seemed slow.

Each setback, each obstacle became an opportunity to exercise patience, to remind myself that true success is built not in a day but through a series of choices, through a dedication to consistency, to quality, to excellence. In moments of doubt, I would remind myself of the purpose that had driven me from the beginning, a purpose that was as much about serving others as it was about achieving success. For in each delay, in each challenge, I saw a reminder of the importance of resilience, a call to approach each day with a heart that was both determined and humble, a heart that trusted in Allah's plan.

With each lesson, I felt a renewed sense of purpose, a commitment to build a business that would bring blessings upon all those who used it, a business that would honor both my ambitions and my faith.

As my app continued to gain traction, I found myself exploring new avenues for growth, new ways to expand, to reach a wider audience, to bring my work to those who could benefit from its features. I began working on new ideas, crafting concepts that would complement my original app, that would offer additional value, that would serve different needs, different audiences. The process of developing these ideas was both challenging and exciting, a journey that required both creativity and discipline, a dedication to build something that was both profitable and meaningful.

In these moments of creation, I felt a renewed sense of purpose, a belief that my journey, though filled with challenges, was one that was blessed, a path that allowed me to grow, to learn, to build something that would bring both success and blessings. Each idea, each concept was a reflection of my journey, a testament to the values that had guided me from the beginning, values of honesty, humility, and compassion.

With each new project, I felt a renewed commitment to ensure that my work, my business, would continue to be a reflection of these values, a platform that would bring blessings upon all those who walked this journey with me, a platform that would honor both my ambitions and my faith.

As my journey unfolded, I found myself in a position to give back, to support those who were less fortunate, to use my blessings in a way that would bring goodness into the lives of others. I began to explore ways to contribute, to build initiatives that would serve the community, to use my success as a means of supporting those who needed it most. This process of giving back became a journey in itself, a path that reminded me of the importance of gratitude, a reminder that my success, though valuable, was also a trust, a responsibility to use my wealth in a way that would bring blessings upon those who were less fortunate.

Each initiative, each contribution was a reflection of my commitment to live in a way that honored both my family and my faith, a way that would bring blessings upon those who walked this journey with me, a way that would ensure that my success would be a source of joy, of gratitude, of blessings for those around me.

With each act of giving, I felt a deep sense of fulfillment, a knowledge that my journey, though filled with ambition, was also a path of service, a chance to use my blessings in a way that would honor both my ambitions and my values.

In the quiet moments of reflection, I found myself thinking about the impact of my work, the legacy I wished to leave, the purpose I wanted my business to fulfill. I understood that my journey, though personal, was also a means of contributing to something greater, a path that allowed me to serve, to uplift, to build a life that would bring both success and blessings upon those around me. Each day, I felt a renewed commitment to ensure that my work would remain aligned with this purpose, a reminder that true success is not measured by wealth alone but by the legacy one leaves, by the kindness one extends, by the blessings one brings into the lives of others.

In moments of doubt, when the challenges felt overwhelming, I would turn to my faith, seeking guidance, strength, and reassurance, a reminder that my journey was not mine alone but a path that required both resilience and humility, a journey that would bring both success and blessings. For in each step forward, I saw a reminder of the purpose that had driven me from the beginning, a purpose that was as much about serving others as it was about achieving success.

With each day, I felt a renewed sense of purpose, a commitment to build a business that would bring both profit and purpose, a reminder that true wealth is measured not by the coins in one's hand but by the goodness in one's heart, by the impact one has upon the lives of others.

In those moments when I stepped back to look upon all that had been built, I realized that true success is as much a state of the heart as it is an accomplishment in the world. This journey had been filled with achievements, with milestones that were visible and measurable, yet I came to understand that the most meaningful rewards were those that could not be weighed or counted. These rewards were found in the joy of serving others, in the fulfillment of building something with purpose, in the quiet peace that came from knowing I had acted with integrity.

As I reflected upon this understanding, I felt a sense of gratitude that was as humbling as it was inspiring. I saw that my work, though challenging, was a gift, a means of contributing, of creating, of serving in a way that would bring blessings upon those who trusted in my vision. This gratitude strengthened my resolve to keep moving forward, to continue refining, improving, and expanding in ways that would honor both my ambitions and my faith. Each day became an opportunity, a reminder of the responsibility I carried, a commitment to ensure that my journey would remain true to its purpose, that my work would bring both profit and blessings.

With each reflection, I felt a renewed sense of purpose, a commitment to build a business that would bring blessings upon all those who walked this journey with me, a business that would reflect the values of honesty, humility, and compassion.

The journey had also taught me the importance of embracing change, of seeing growth as a process of adaptation, of understanding that each season brings with it new opportunities, new challenges, new lessons. In the early days, I had a vision of what my app could be, a vision that was as ambitious as it was precise. Yet as my work evolved, as I received feedback, as I learned from the experiences of others, I saw that growth requires flexibility, a willingness to adapt, a readiness to see beyond one's own plans and to embrace the unfolding possibilities.

I learned to see change not as a disruption but as an opportunity, a chance to refine, to improve, to build something that was dynamic, that was responsive, that would meet the needs of those it served in a way that was both relevant and meaningful. Each adjustment, each refinement became a reminder of the importance of humility, a call to approach each step with a heart that was open to new ideas, to different perspectives, to the wisdom of those who had walked this path before me.

In moments of uncertainty, I would turn to my faith, seeking guidance, strength, and reassurance, a reminder that my journey was not mine alone but a path that required both resilience and humility, a path that would bring both success and blessings, a path that would reflect the values of Islam.

With each day, I came to understand that my journey, though filled with challenges, was one that was blessed, a gift that allowed me to serve, to contribute, to build something that would bring both success and blessings. My work became a means of expressing gratitude, a chance to honor the blessings that had brought me here, a reminder that true success is measured not by wealth alone but by the legacy of kindness, of compassion, of service that one leaves behind. In each feature, in each function, I saw a reminder of the values that had guided me from the beginning, values of honesty, humility, and service.

In moments of reflection, I would find myself looking ahead, envisioning the future I wished to build, the impact I hoped my work would have, the ways in which my journey might inspire others, uplift them, encourage them to pursue their own paths of purpose, of service, of success. For in each step forward, I saw a reminder of the journey that had brought me to this point, a journey that had been filled with lessons, with moments of growth, with reminders that true success is measured not by wealth alone but by the impact one has upon the lives of others, by the blessings one brings into the lives of those who walk this journey with us.

With each step, I felt a renewed commitment to use my work in a way that would bring blessings upon all those who trusted in my vision, who supported my journey, who walked this path with me.

CHAPTER 10: GRATITUDE AND GIVING BACK

As I stood on the pinnacle of all that had been achieved, I found myself reflecting on the journey that had brought me here, a journey that had been filled with trials, with triumphs, with moments of growth, of gratitude, of grace. Looking back upon my life, from the humble beginnings of my childhood to the present-day success of my ventures, I saw not only a path of ambition but a path of blessings, a road guided by wisdom, by resilience, by faith. It was in those quiet hours of reflection that I understood the true weight of my journey, the purpose that had driven me from the beginning, the calling that had shaped my path.

I saw that my life, though marked by accomplishments, was also a testament to the power of humility, of gratitude, of a heart that had trusted in Allah's plan, that had believed in the goodness of the journey even when the road had seemed uncertain. Each step forward, each lesson learned had brought me closer to a life that was as much about service as it was about success, a life that sought not only to achieve but to honor, to give, to uplift. And as I stood in the quiet of this reflection, I felt a renewed commitment to ensure that my journey, though personal, would also be a means of giving back, a path that would bring blessings upon all those who had walked it with me.

For true success, I realized, is measured not by the wealth one accumulates but by the goodness one brings into the world, by the legacy of kindness, of compassion, of service that one leaves behind.

In these moments of reflection, I felt a profound sense of gratitude for Allah's guidance, a knowledge that my journey, though challenging, was one that had been blessed, a path that had been shaped by a wisdom far greater than my own. From the earliest days, I had seen signs, moments that had reminded me of Allah's presence, of His mercy, of His kindness, moments that had strengthened my faith, that had reminded me that my success was not mine alone but a gift, a blessing, a trust that I had been given. For every obstacle overcome, every milestone achieved, every lesson learned, I saw the hand of Allah, a reminder that my journey was one that had been guided, that had been protected, that had been blessed.

This realization filled me with a deep sense of humility, a reminder that my work, though valuable, was also a trust, a responsibility to use my blessings in a way that would honor both my ambitions and my faith, a way that would bring blessings upon those around me. Each success became an opportunity to express gratitude, to recognize the blessings that had brought me here, to ensure that my journey would be a means of giving back, a path that would reflect the values of Islam, values of honesty, humility, and compassion.

With each prayer, I felt a renewed sense of gratitude for Allah's guidance, a reminder that my journey, though personal, was a path that allowed me to serve, to give, to bring blessings upon all those who walked this journey with me.

As I reflected upon the lessons I had learned, I saw that my journey was not merely about achieving success but about cultivating a spirit of learning, a heart that was open, a mind that was willing to grow, to adapt, to evolve. Success, I realized, is not a destination but a journey, a path that requires continuous learning, a commitment to remain humble, to remain open, to see each day as an opportunity to grow, to learn, to improve. I understood that true success requires humility, a willingness to see one's own limitations, a readiness to seek wisdom, to learn from others, to adapt to new challenges.

With each lesson learned, I felt a renewed commitment to approach my work with humility, with a heart that was both open and discerning, a heart that sought not only to achieve but to grow, to improve, to refine. For in each lesson, in each moment of growth, I saw a reminder of the importance of humility, a call to approach each day with a heart that was willing to learn, to grow, to build a life that would bring both success and blessings upon all those who walked this journey with me.

With each step forward, I felt a renewed sense of gratitude for the lessons I had learned, a reminder that my journey, though challenging, was one that was blessed, a path that allowed me to grow, to serve, to build something meaningful.

In moments of reflection, I felt a renewed commitment to give back, to use my blessings in a way that would bring goodness into the lives of others, to ensure that my journey, though filled with ambition, would also be a path of service, a means of supporting those who were less fortunate. I came to understand the importance of Zakat, the obligation to give, to support, to uplift those in need, a practice that was as much about gratitude as it was about generosity. Through Zakat, I saw a way to honor the blessings I had received, a way to share the fruits of my success, a way to bring blessings upon all those who walked this journey with me.

Each act of giving became a reminder of the importance of compassion, a call to live in a way that honored both my family and my faith, a way that would bring blessings upon those who needed it most, a way that would ensure that my success would be a source of joy, of gratitude, of blessings for those around me. In these moments, I felt a renewed sense of purpose, a commitment to give back, to support, to contribute to something greater, to build a life that would bring both success and blessings upon those who walked this journey with me.

For in each act of giving, I saw a reminder of the journey that had brought me here, a journey that had been filled with blessings, with lessons, with moments of grace.

With each blessing, with each success, I felt a renewed desire to share my story, to open up about the journey I had walked, the lessons I had learned, the purpose that had driven me from the beginning. I wanted to inspire others, especially young Muslims, to pursue their dreams, to build lives of purpose, to seek success in a way that was halal, in a way that would honor both their ambitions and their faith. For in each story, I saw a reflection of my journey, a testament to the power of faith, of resilience, of a heart that had trusted in Allah's plan.

Through my words, I hoped to uplift, to encourage, to remind others that their dreams were possible, that their journeys, though filled with challenges, were also paths of blessings, of grace, of growth. I felt a deep sense of gratitude for the opportunity to share, a reminder that my journey, though personal, was also a means of giving, a path that allowed me to bring blessings upon those who walked this journey with me.

With each story shared, I felt a renewed sense of purpose, a commitment to use my voice in a way that would bring blessings upon those who heard it, a voice that would inspire, that would uplift, that would bring goodness into the lives of those who walked this journey with me.

As I continued to share my story, I felt a deep commitment to encourage halal wealth creation, to advocate for a form of success that was grounded in Islamic principles, in ethics, in a dedication to serve, to uplift, to contribute to something greater. I understood that wealth, when pursued with honesty, with humility, with a commitment to remain true to one's values, is a blessing, a gift that brings both success and purpose, a reminder that true wealth is measured not by the coins in one's hand but by the goodness in one's heart, by the impact one has upon the lives of others.

Through my work, I sought to inspire others to build lives of purpose, to pursue success in a way that was both profitable and meaningful, a way that would bring blessings upon all those who walked this journey with me. I felt a renewed sense of gratitude for the opportunity to share, a reminder that my journey, though personal, was also a means of giving, a path that allowed me to bring blessings upon those who walked this journey with me.

With each message, I felt a renewed sense of purpose, a commitment to use my work in a way that would bring blessings upon all those who trusted in my vision, a way that would honor both my ambitions and my faith.

With each passing day, I found myself deepening my understanding of what it meant to use wealth as a means of fulfilling a greater purpose. The blessings I had received were not simply a reward for my work but a trust, a responsibility to use these gifts in a way that would bring goodness, that would reflect the values that had shaped my journey. This trust was a reminder that wealth, in its truest form, is not a treasure to be kept but a resource to be shared, a tool that allows one to uplift, to support, to contribute to a world that is kinder, more compassionate, more just.

In this spirit, I began to explore initiatives that would allow me to give back to my community, to support those who were less fortunate, to ensure that my journey, though personal, would also be a source of blessings for those around me. I reached out to local organizations, to charities, to those who were working tirelessly to improve the lives of others, to offer my support, my resources, my commitment to help them in their mission. Each contribution, each act of giving became a reminder of the blessings I had received, a reflection of the values of compassion, of humility, of service.

For in each act of giving, I saw a reflection of my journey, a testament to the power of faith, of resilience, of a heart that had trusted in Allah's plan, a heart that believed in the goodness of the journey.

As I continued to give back, I began to understand the importance of consistency, of building a habit of generosity, a practice of giving that would be as natural as breathing, as essential as the work I had done to build my business. I came to see that true generosity is not a single act but a lifestyle, a commitment to use one's blessings in a way that would bring lasting goodness, a way that would honor both one's ambitions and one's faith. Each day, as I dedicated time to these initiatives, as I contributed my resources, my time, my energy, I felt a deep sense of fulfillment, a knowledge that my journey, though filled with ambition, was also a path of service.

This habit of giving became a cornerstone of my life, a reminder that true success is not measured by wealth alone but by the legacy one leaves, by the kindness one extends, by the blessings one brings into the lives of those around them. In moments of reflection, I felt a renewed commitment to live in a way that honored both my family and my faith, a way that would bring blessings upon all those who walked this journey with me, a way that would ensure that my success would be a source of joy, of gratitude, of blessings for those around me.

With each act of giving, I felt a renewed sense of purpose, a commitment to use my wealth in a way that would bring goodness into the lives of others, a way that would reflect the values of Islam, values of honesty, humility, and compassion.

In addition to giving financially, I felt a strong desire to share the lessons I had learned, to offer guidance to those who were just beginning their journeys, to support young entrepreneurs who were navigating the same challenges I had faced. I understood that my journey, though personal, was also a story that could inspire, that could uplift, that could offer hope to those who might be struggling, who might be searching for purpose, for direction, for a path that would bring both success and blessings. Through mentorship, I found a new way to give back, a way to offer not only resources but wisdom, insight, encouragement.

I began to meet with aspiring entrepreneurs, young minds filled with ambition, with dreams, with visions of success, of purpose, of lives that would bring value to the world. In these meetings, I shared my story, the lessons I had learned, the mistakes I had made, the values that had guided me, values of honesty, humility, and service. I encouraged them to pursue their dreams with a heart that was both ambitious and humble, a heart that trusted in Allah's plan, a heart that believed in the goodness of the journey.

For in each word, in each story, I saw a reminder of the journey that had brought me here, a journey that had been filled with blessings, with lessons, with moments of grace.

Through mentorship, I came to see the power of connection, the importance of community, the strength that comes from sharing, from supporting, from encouraging others on their journeys. I understood that my success, though valuable, was also a means of building a community, a network of individuals who believed in the same values, who shared the same purpose, who sought to build lives of meaning, of purpose, of service. This community became a source of joy, a reminder that my journey, though personal, was also a shared vision, a path that allowed me to connect, to build relationships, to create a legacy of kindness, of compassion, of service.

With each interaction, I felt a renewed commitment to ensure that my work, my journey, would continue to be a reflection of the values that had shaped my life, a reflection of the principles of honesty, of humility, of compassion. I saw my community as a family, a network of individuals who supported one another, who encouraged one another, who believed in the power of faith, of resilience, of a heart that trusted in Allah's plan.

With each day, I felt a renewed sense of purpose, a commitment to build a community that would bring blessings upon all those who walked this journey with me, a community that would honor both my ambitions and my faith.

In moments of reflection, I often found myself expressing gratitude for the support, the encouragement, the belief of those who had been part of my journey, who had offered their insights, their time, their friendship. My friends Aman and Maqsood, who had walked this path with me, became my brothers in spirit, my companions in this journey of purpose, of service, of success. Together, we celebrated each success, each milestone, each achievement with gratitude, with a commitment to remain humble, to ensure that our work would continue to bring value, to serve, to uplift, to honor both our ambitions and our values.

In their presence, I felt a sense of joy, a reminder that true success is a shared journey, a blessing that grows when it is given, a gift that brings not only wealth but meaning, fulfillment, a sense of purpose that goes beyond profit, beyond achievement. I felt a renewed commitment to use my blessings in a way that would honor both my family and my faith, a way that would bring blessings upon all those who walked this journey with me, a way that would ensure that my success would be a source of joy, of gratitude, of blessings for those around me.

With each day, I felt a renewed sense of purpose, a commitment to build a life that would bring both success and blessings upon all those who walked this journey with me.

As I continued to give back, I came to see that true wealth is measured not by the treasures one possesses but by the goodness one brings into the world, by the kindness one extends, by the blessings one bestows upon those around them. I understood that wealth, when pursued with integrity, with a commitment to remain true to one's values, becomes a blessing, a gift that allows one to build a life that is both profitable and meaningful, a life that reflects the values of Islam, values of honesty, humility, and service. In moments of reflection, I felt a renewed commitment to live in a way that would honor both my ambitions and my faith, a way that would bring blessings upon all those who walked this journey with me.

With each act of giving, each moment of gratitude, I felt a deep sense of fulfillment, a knowledge that my journey, though filled with ambition, was also a path of service, a reminder that true success is not measured by wealth alone but by the impact one has upon the lives of others, by the blessings one brings into the lives of those who walk this journey with us.

With each step forward, I felt a renewed commitment to ensure that my journey, though personal, would also be a means of giving, a path that allowed me to bring blessings upon all those who walked this journey with me, a path that would honor both my family and my faith.

As the journey continued, I felt compelled to deepen my involvement in causes that resonated with my values. I understood that true success was measured not only by achievements but by the ability to make a lasting impact, to support endeavors that uplifted others. I began reaching out to educational programs, especially those that supported young, underprivileged students, offering scholarships and resources that would give them the foundation they needed to pursue their dreams. I saw this as an opportunity to inspire a new generation, to remind them that with faith, resilience, and hard work, they too could achieve greatness, that they too could build lives filled with purpose.

In supporting these students, I felt a deep connection to my own journey, to the humble beginnings that had shaped my life, to the challenges I had faced and overcome. I understood that each act of support, each resource shared was a means of honoring those who had supported me, those who had believed in me, those who had offered their encouragement, their wisdom, their love. I saw in these young students a reflection of my own aspirations, a reminder of the dreams that had driven me, the purpose that had guided me.

With each act of support, I felt a renewed sense of purpose, a commitment to use my blessings in a way that would bring goodness into the lives of others, a way that would reflect the values of Islam, values of honesty, humility, and compassion.

In these acts of giving, I came to understand the profound joy that comes from serving others, a joy that goes beyond wealth, beyond success, a joy that is rooted in the heart, in the knowledge that one's actions have made a difference, that one's journey has brought blessings upon others. I saw that true fulfillment was found not in the accolades or the achievements but in the quiet satisfaction of knowing that my work, my journey, had been a means of bringing joy, of offering hope, of building a legacy of kindness, of compassion, of service.

Through these experiences, I felt a renewed commitment to live a life that would honor both my ambitions and my faith, a life that would be as much about giving as it was about achieving, a life that would bring blessings upon all those who walked this journey with me. Each day became an opportunity to express gratitude, to share, to give, to build a legacy that would inspire others, that would remind them of the importance of humility, of generosity, of a heart that seeks to serve, to uplift, to bring goodness into the lives of others.

With each reflection, I felt a deep sense of gratitude for the blessings I had received, a reminder that my journey, though personal, was also a means of giving, a path that allowed me to bring blessings upon all those who walked this journey with me, a path that would honor both my family and my faith.

ABOUT THE AUTHOR

Afjal Khan is a dedicated writer, educator, and student of Islamic sciences, passionate about guiding Muslim parents in raising their children with strong Islamic values amidst the challenges of modern, secular society. Deeply committed to nurturing the spiritual and moral development of families, his work is rooted in the authentic teachings of the Qur'an and Sunnah, offering practical and actionable advice for Muslim parents seeking to build a strong Islamic foundation for their children.

Drawing inspiration from the rich legacy of the **Salaf** and emphasizing the core principles of **Tawheed** and Islamic upbringing, Afjal Khan seeks to empower parents to instill a deep love for Islam within their children. He emphasizes the cultivation of resilience, humility, and a strong sense of Islamic identity, all while navigating the pressures and complexities of contemporary society. Through his work, he aims to bridge the gap between timeless Islamic values and the realities of modern-day parenting.

"As a humble student of knowledge, I **(Afjal Khan)** welcome any feedback or corrections. While I strive to ensure that everything I share aligns with the Qur'an and Sunnah, I am human and capable of making mistakes. If any part of my work inadvertently contradicts authentic Islamic teachings, I ask for your forgiveness. Please do not follow my words if they conflict with Islam, and I kindly request that you inform me of any errors so that I may correct them, inshaAllah, as long as I am alive. You are welcome to reach out to me at **mdafjalkhan29@gmail.com** for any corrections, insights, or questions."

Afjal Khan's writing is deeply rooted in the authentic traditions of Islam, while also addressing the unique challenges faced by Muslim parents today. His mission is to reconnect families with the essence of Islam, helping them cultivate faith, character, and a deep connection to Allah in every aspect of life. Whether through his books, lectures, or online content, Afjal Khan remains committed to supporting families as they strive to raise righteous, resilient, and faithful children in a world that often challenges their beliefs.

To stay connected with **Afjal Khan** and access valuable insights, free eBooks, and resources designed to strengthen your understanding of Islamic parenting, join his community. As a special thank you for joining, you'll receive an

@IQRAJOURNEY

exclusive guide to help you on your journey of raising righteous Muslim children.

www.ingramcontent.com/pod-product-compliance
Lightning Source LLC
Chambersburg PA
CBHW070241220526
45465CB00004B/1480